The Juice Book

Gwyneth Dover appears regularly on television and has been featured on *TVam*, *Bazaar*, *Lifestyle Television* and the *Miriam Stoppard Show*. Her previous books are *Diet for Life*, *The New Diet for Life*, *Entertaining with Gwyneth Dover* and *Sweets without Sinning*. Gwyneth has also been featured on many radio programmes and has lectured on disease prevention, fitness and health alongside top heart surgeons, quite apart from giving cookery demonstrations all over Britain. In 1989 she was invited by the *Daily Telegraph* to act as diet and health expert for their pre-retirement cruises and in 1991 was fitness, diet and health lecturer for the CTC Canary Cruise.

With her husband Richard she won the 'Here's to Health' award in 1987. They live in a farmhouse in North Yorkshire which they converted themselves.

GWYNETH DOVER

The Juice Book

RECIPES FOR HEALTH AND BEAUTY

PAN BOOKS

LONDON, SYDNEY AND AUCKLAND

First published 1993 by
PAN BOOKS LIMITED
a division of Pan Macmillan Publishers Limited
Cavaye Place London SW10 9PG
and Basingstoke

Associated companies throughout the world

ISBN 0 330 33051 9

1 3 5 7 9 8 6 4 2

A CIP catalogue record for this book is available from
the British Library

Photoset by Parker Typesetting Service, Leicester
Printed and bound in Great Britain by
Mackays of Chatham PLC, Chatham, Kent

CONTENTS

INTRODUCTION

S o you are the proud owner of a juicing machine and you have probably made a few fruit juices since buying it. But now it sits, quite unceremoniously, on some shelf gathering dust. Well, now is the time to give it pride of place in your kitchen and start juicing regularly each and every day. It's amazing how quickly you will notice the difference in yourself. As you reap the benefits of juicing you will feel much healthier and fitter, with more energy and vitality than you know what to do with. And you will look better than ever before – naturally.

You may ask, 'Why not simply buy fruit and vegetable juices from a shop instead of making them?' The answer is simple: home-made juices are totally different from the shop-bought varieties on a number of counts.

Firstly, the taste and texture of your own juices are far superior – there really is no comparison at all.

Secondly, the juices you concoct are pure and natural and you know exactly what is in them. That is not necessarily the case with shop-bought versions. Quite often the manufacturers use various additives and preservatives in their juices which we would prefer to avoid for health reasons.

Thirdly, from a nutritional standpoint, the shop-bought juices are grossly inferior to your own. When you make your own juices you can ensure that the produce used is the freshest possible and of a good quality, thereby maximizing the nutrients. The fruits and vegetables used for manufactured juices are usually of a poor quality, often bruised or damaged in some way, making them unsuitable for supermarket shelves but fine for being juiced and hidden in containers. Freshness isn't of prime importance though, when you consider that these juices are in effect 'cooked' by the processing method, which largely destroys the vitamins and minerals. Shop-bought juices are far less valuable in terms of the all-important nutrients present.

1

Lastly, experimenting with various combinations of fruits and vegetables will result in some deliciously different juices which you would never be able to buy in a shop. Just think of the variety available to you. You can have a tailor-made juicing programme.

The beauty of making your own juices and bombarding your body with all those concentrated nutrients is that it takes only minutes from start to finish. Juices are the ultimate in fast food! And with our hectic lifestyles the time element involved is of prime importance. All you have to do is wash the produce, pop it into the machine, juice it and drink it.

Juicing is also fun. The whole family can get involved. Children, especially, love to see their favourite fruit and vegetables go into one part of the machine and bright juice come out of another. Then there's the fun of tasting it and planning your next delicious and unique juice. I am convinced that you will enjoy the juicing experience just as much as I do.

Happy juicing!

Note: All quantities given in the recipes sections yield approximately one glass of juice, but note that quantities can vary depending on the size of the fruit and vegetables used.

CHAPTER ONE

SO WHAT CAN JUICING DO FOR YOU?

D rinking juice is the perfect natural extension to following a healthy diet. Anyone who is remotely interested in their health or the health of their family should be juicing fresh fruit and vegetables every day to achieve optimum health and beauty.

I have always believed in the statement 'You are what you eat'. If you consume mainly junk food laden with saturated fat, sugars, salt and chemicals, how can you expect your body to be fit and healthy, and to thrive? Quite simply, you can't, and it won't. Just like a car that has been neglected and not been given the correct fuel, the system breaks down sooner or later.

But why juice when you can simply eat fruit and vegetables? Juices are concentrated forms of the nutrients contained in the fruit and vegetables. By juicing the nutrients are extracted from the fibre, a job normally conducted by your digestive system. It would be impractical to consume the same amount of vitamins and minerals from the whole raw produce. One cup of carrot juice will give you the same nutrients as contained in four cups of the raw chopped vegetable. You would need to consume 1 lb, or 500 g, of raw celery to gain the nutrients from one cup of this juice. I know which method I prefer! Just think of the amount of raw produce you would have to consume to obtain such high nutrient intakes. Another great advantage of juicing is that because it is already in a liquid form the body can skip a stage in the digestive process and the nutrients are absorbed effectively and efficiently straight away. And you can mix your juices to ensure your optimum nutrient levels.

We all know that the consumption of fresh fruit and vegetables is vitally important to our health. Eaten whole, they are an excellent source of fibre. Now worldwide research is increasingly showing the protective role offered by the rich supply of vitamins and minerals they possess. This is where juicing comes in. Many of their health-giving qualities have been known for centuries. Scientists, the medical profession and various health organizations are becoming more aware of the benefits as research reinforces the qualities of these ancient remedies.

The major killer diseases that ravage our society, such as cancer, heart disease, high blood pressure and strokes, may be preventable. Evidence suggests that the symptoms of diseases and ailments ranging from arthritis to the common cold, from insomnia to lack of energy, can be ameliorated by consuming vitamin and mineral packed juices.

Adding juice to your life will make a great difference to your health both in the short and long term. You will feel vibrant, alive, and bursting with energy and vitality.

Chapters 3 and 4 list for you alphabetically the fruits and vegetables which I find particularly useful for juicing. Their nutritional values and medicinal powers are given to enable you to devise your very own unique juice plan. You can't go wrong with all that information available to you!

Chapter 6 looks at how you can have clearer, smoother, younger looking skin which is free from blemish, how your hair can become stronger, thicker and shinier, your nails longer and stronger, and your eyes bright, sparkling and clear.

Everyone is concerned to some extent about how they look, and I'm sure we all want to look as good as we possibly can – I know I do. The very best thing you can do to enhance your natural beauty is to get into the juicing habit. All you have to do to give your natural beauty a boost is to consume juices containing, amongst other things, the all-important nutrients silicon and selenium – the youth-givers. Try the recipes I have devised and then experiment with your own, and just watch your beauty bloom. It's so nice when people start to comment on how good you look and it's even nicer when they want to know what your secret is!

And what about your sex life? Could that do with a little help?

Chapter 7 shows how juices can benefit you in the bedroom as well! Aphrodisiacs have been known for centuries and throughout many civilizations, especially ancient Greece and Rome. Once again modern day research tends to confirm the qualities of these sex enhancers. Celery is just one example. It was popular in eighteenth-century France for its powers of increasing sexual desire and performance. Today, researchers have found it contains pheromones, a substance which stimulates the sex senses. The mineral zinc has been found to be very beneficial for men experiencing impotency. Juicing with fruit and vegetables which contain nutrients associated with stimulating the sexual act can only work in your favour.

Chapters 8–12 look at the various diseases and ailments most common in our society today: cancer, heart disease, strokes, high blood pressure, digestive problems and stress-related ailments, plus many more. I recommend the nutrients which have been shown to be of benefit in the prevention and treatment of such health problems. Each section contains many delicious recipes for you to try. But, more than this, the information is there for you to concoct your own delicious juices.

Consuming juices as a natural way of life will also help you to lose unwanted weight and inches. That has to be good news when the majority of us have too much padding on our skeletons. The reason for this is simple. Fruit and vegetables are low in calories, jam-packed full of nutrients and satisfy your sweet tooth as well as making you feel adequately full. A large glass of fruit juice contains about a hundred calories and vegetable juice a mere fifty.

I am not in favour of dieting as such because in the end you put more weight back on than you lost in the first place. That is scientific fact. Diets do not work. The only way to lose weight and keep that weight off is to change your long-term eating habits. Juicing helps you to do this by getting your tastebuds used to fat-free, natural-tasting fruit and vegetables. You are obtaining all the vitamins and minerals your body needs which, amongst other things, maintains your energy levels. By eating light, low-fat meals alongside the juicing regime you cannot help but shed those surplus pounds and inches.

Do you need any more convincing about the virtues of juicing? I certainly don't!

CHAPTER TWO

THE POWER OF
NUTRIENTS

B y nutrients I mean vitamins and minerals; they are absolutely essential in achieving and maintaining good health. Without them the body cannot develop and grow normally and deficiency symptoms occur as the system becomes increasingly susceptible to disease. The power of nutrients has been grossly underestimated in the past. However, thanks to recent research, vitamins and minerals are being seen in a totally new light, not just by naturopaths and homoeopaths, but by the mainstream medical profession.

Vitamins are made by bacteria, plants or animals. Our bodies cannot manufacture all the vitamins we require, or in sufficient quantities, so our diet must supplement the supply. The foods you eat are the main source of minerals as these are not manufactured by the body at all. It's fortunate that we can gain sufficient nutrients in vegetables, fruit, grains and legumes. Taking vitamin and mineral supplements is unnecessary except in exceptional circumstances and really only results in very expensive urine.

Let's take a closer look at the various vitamins and minerals and the role each one plays within our bodies. By applying this knowledge we can gain optimum health and beauty by the juicing method.

Vital Vitamins

Scientists only discovered the existence of vitamins in 1912, but many civilizations have been very much aware of their properties for centuries. Fifteen thousand years before the birth of Christ, the ancient Egyptians found that night blindness could be cured if they ate foods rich in vitamin A, also known as beta-carotene. During the mid-eighteenth century, sailors were given rations of lemon juice on their voyages to help combat the onset of scurvy.

Common diseases associated with undernutrition, such as rickets, beri beri and pellagra, have been eliminated in the western world thanks to a diet which is rich in vitamins.

Vitamins can be divided into two distinct categories – fat soluble and water soluble. Vitamins A, D, E and K are fat soluble and are stored in the body to be used when required. Because they are stored rather than excreted poisonous build-ups can develop. The B complex vitamins and vitamin C are water soluble. Water soluble vitamins, except vitamin B_{12} and folic acid, are not stored and must be consumed on a regular daily basis, as any excess is excreted in the urine.

FAT SOLUBLE VITAMINS

VITAMIN A

Vitamin A is sometimes known by its chemical name, retinol. You will not find vitamin A in any known fruit or vegetable in the world as it is only found in foods of animal origin. However, its active precursor, beta-carotene, is present in certain fruits and vegetables and when this is consumed the body converts it into vitamin A.

Vitamin A is toxic and dangerous in excess, but it is virtually impossible to overdose from diet alone – unless you are partial to polar bear, whale or shark liver! Overdose occurs when people supplement their diet with pills, potions and fish oil capsules. Excess intake results in poor appetite, hair loss, headaches and peeling itchy skin. Once the dosage is reduced, the symptoms disappear, but long-term damage can occur in children. But don't worry, gaining your vitamin A from its natural sources of fruit and vegetables cannot cause intoxication. Juicing enables you to gain from all the benefits vitamin A can bring without having to worry about the toxic effects.

The functions of vitamin A are numerous and include helping to maintain a strong immune system, maintaining the health of the skin and hair, and improving colour and night vision. It is also necessary for growth, bones and teeth. It helps to protect against various forms of cancer and is one of the vitamins leading the fight against the ageing process.

If your diet is lacking in vitamin A then you may suffer deficiency symptoms which could include poor sight, burning and itching eyes, dry eyes, eye ulceration, poor hair and skin quality, respiratory infections, depression, rickets and bone softening.

The best sources of beta-carotene are found in yellow or orange and green vegetables such as carrots, kale, spinach and squash.

Rich sources of beta-carotene:

FRUITS		VEGETABLES	
apples	grapes	beetroot	courgettes
apricots	peaches	broccoli	cucumbers
blackberries	pineapples	cabbage	kale
cantaloup	plums	carrots	lettuce
melons	raspberries	cauliflower	onions
cranberries	strawberries	celery	spinach
	watermelons		squash
			sweet potatoes
			tomatoes
			watercress

You should have no problem at all in making sure that you have sufficient beta-carotene in your juices.

VITAMIN D

Vitamin D is the sunshine vitamin. It is so called because this vitamin is produced by the skin when it is exposed to sunlight. It is necessary for the absorption of calcium from food and the hardening of the bones and teeth along with calcium and phosphorus. If you have insufficient amounts of vitamin D it results in rickets during child-hood and osteomalacia in adulthood, along with muscle weakness and spasms.

Vitamin D is the most toxic of all vitamins

So for once we can say that it's actually good for you to expose your skin to sunshine, but do still use suntan preparations. Walking, sitting on a park bench, gardening, exercising in the open air, are all excellent ways of ensuring your daily dose of vitamin D. And the more of your body you expose, the more vitamin D is produced.

Fruits and vegetables do not contain any vitamin D – in fact, very few foods do and then it is limited to those of animal origin.

Overdose with vitamin D results in loss of appetite, nausea, vomiting, constant thirst, head pains and children may become very depressed, irritable and thin. Adults are less susceptible to overdose than children.

VITAMIN E

Vitamin E has increasingly become known as the 'miracle' vitamin, reputed to cure a variety of conditions varying from heart disease to sexual problems, from wrinkles to cancer.

Vitamin E is held in the membranes of cells and is essential for maintaining their orderly structure and for normal metabolism. This vitamin is also an antioxidant of polyunsaturated fatty acids in cell membranes and the bloodstream which guards against cardio-vascular disease and strokes. Vitamin E is important as an anti-blood-clotting agent and a blood-vessel dilator as well as maintaining healthy blood vessels. It is valuable in the fight against cholesterol, increasing the safe HDL type and reducing the LDL type (*see* page 91). Vitamin E also protects vitamin A and promotes the ability of white blood cells to resist infection. It is also thought to accelerate wound healing from burns or accidents and to lessen scarring. Vitamin E is claimed to be a sex enhancer, increasing virility and protecting against sterility in men.

Compared with vitamins A and D, vitamin E is said to be harmless in large amounts. Symptoms of excess intake would include nausea, diarrhoea, palpitations and muscle weakness. As

9

vitamin E is so important in the structure of cell membranes, a lack of this vitamin can have profound effects especially on the nervous system. Other symptoms include walking difficulties, changes in the eye, loss of touch or pain sensations, muscle weakness, lethargy, apathy, irritability, decreased vitality and lack of sexual interest. But, because body stores of vitamin E are so large, these deficiency symptoms are quite rare and only emerge in those with metabolism problems or difficulties in absorbing fat from food.

Good sources of vitamin E include broccoli, carrots, celery and leafy green vegetables.

Vitamin K

The sole proven function of vitamin K is in the control of blood clotting, though there is some evidence to suggest that this vitamin aids the healing of fractures and may also have a part to play in preventing osteoporosis. We are not totally dependent on dietary supplies of vitamin K as it is synthesized by bacteria in the digestive system. Most vitamin K in the diet is supplied by vegetables, with cabbage, sprouts, cauliflower and spinach probably being the richest sources. Adult deficiency is unlikely, but newborn babies are susceptible to vitamin K deficiency in the first few days of life as they have no bacteria inhabiting the digestive system and milk is a poor source. Natural sources of vitamin K are not thought to be toxic when taken in excess and there are no known symptoms of overdose with this vitamin.

Drink a good supply of juices containing dark leafy green vegetables to ensure your vitamin K level is adequate.

WATER SOLUBLE VITAMINS

The Vitamin B Complex

The B complex is a mixture of vitamins that tend to occur together in foods of plant, animal and micro-organism origin. There are eight true vitamins in the complex: B_1 (thiamin), B_2 (riboflavin), B_3 (niacin or nicotinic acid), B_5 (pantothenic acid), B_6 (pyridoxine), biotin, folic acid and B_{12} (cobalamin). Sometimes you may find choline and inositol included, but they can be synthesized by the body.

Chemical substances also form a part of the B complex. These are not strictly speaking vitamins, but factors and are called PABA, para-aminobenzoic acid, pangamic acid and laetrite.

All the B complex vitamins have different chemical structures and different, though related, functions in the body. Probably the most important function of the complex is in metabolizing carbohydrates, fats and proteins. As such it is strongly associated with our energy levels and athletic performance. Many leading athletes concentrate on the B complex vitamins to enhance their performance. This group of vitamins is also useful in achieving a healthy skin and hair.

Leafy greens and sprouts are amongst the best sources of the vitamin B complex.

B_1 (THIAMIN)   Thiamin is absolutely essential for growth and life. It is necessary for many metabolic processes, especially the release of energy from glucose. It also assists in the efficient transmission of messages to the brain. Thiamin therefore keeps us mentally healthy, alert and neurologically fit. This vitamin has also been found useful in the treatment of anaemia and diabetes.

It is the nervous system that is affected first by the deficiency of thiamin. Initial symptoms are weight loss due to vomiting, nausea, insomnia, depression, irritability and lack of concentration. Symptoms then develop into degeneration of the nerves and atrophy of the muscles they supply, along with memory loss. Beri beri is the classic nervous disorder caused by thiamin deficiency. These days it is rare except amongst alcoholics and this is because alcohol interferes with thiamin absorption. This vitamin cannot be stored by the body and any excesses are filtered out of the bloodstream by the kidneys to be passed out of the body as urine.

Thiamin is found in plant life and a really good source is the Brussels sprout.

B_2 (RIBOFLAVIN)   Riboflavin is present in nearly all foods except sugar, fats and spirits, and is needed for healthy skin and eyes. It is essential for many processes, especially the release of energy from food. The need for the vitamin varies from person to person and it is related to the number of active non-fat cells in the body. Athletes and others with highly developed muscles will require more riboflavin than someone who takes little exercise. Anyone who exercises strenuously will find riboflavin beneficial as it increases performance. It is also thought to be effective in guarding against some forms of cancer and anaemia. No symptoms of excessive intake have been reported, as it is filtered out of the body and passed as urine – but it may turn urine bright yellow which is harmless, if somewhat disconcerting! In fact, it is so safe that it is used as a food colouring.

Lack of riboflavin affects growth in children, but does not seem to seriously affect adults. The only symptoms are a sore, magenta tongue, eczema around the nose, chin and groin and eyes which are bloodshot and sensitive to light.

Good sources of riboflavin are found in green vegetables such as broccoli, spinach and spring greens. The Kiwi fruit is also a useful supplier of this vitamin.

B_3 (NIACIN)   Also known as nicotinic acid, niacin is the group name for two forms of the vitamin – niacin and nicotinamide. These two co-enzymes are involved in the liberation of energy within cells and producing energy from sugars, fats and proteins. This vitamin is also important in maintaining healthy skin, nerves, brain, tongue and digestive system.

Its main therapeutic use is in reducing cholesterol levels in the blood and guarding against cardiovascular disease and high blood pressure. Arthritis sufferers have also found relief from this vitamin. Deficiency symptoms include dermatitis, diarrhoea and pellagra, resulting in dementia, loss of appetite, nauseau and vomiting, inflamed mouth, insomnia, irritability, stress and depression.

Nicotinamide is harmless when taken in excess as it is filtered out by the kidneys and excreted in the urine. Niacin overdose sometimes causes flushing and a burning sensation in the head, neck and arms, headaches, dry skin and abdominal cramps.

Niacin is found in leafy greens, vegetables and Brussels sprouts.

B_6 (PYRIDOXINE)   Pyridoxine is essential for growth, body repair, blood formation, healthy skin and nerves, as well as protection against infection. It boosts the immune system and gives us extra energy. This vitamin is also very useful as an anti-depressant especially in the treatment of pre-menstrual tension, and for morning and travel sickness.

A diet lacking in pyridoxine will show the symptoms of an inflamed tongue, splitting lips, puffy ankles and fingers, irritability and depression, migraine, anaemia and arteriosclerosis.

Mega-doses of supplements, several grams per day, of pyridoxin have resulted in damage to the nervous system shown by an unstable gait, and loss of sensation in the hands, legs and feet. Symptoms cease soon after the vitamin is withdrawn.

Good sources of pyridoxine are avocado pears, bananas, bean sprouts, beans, broccoli, cauliflower and peas.

B_{12} (COBALAMIN)   This is known as the anti-pernicious anaemia vitamin because deficiency results in the disease. Symptoms of deficiency include a smooth, sore tongue, nerve degeneration and menstrual disorders.

Cobalamin performs various functions in the body, including maintaining a healthy nervous system, building the genetic material DNA and helping in the formation of red blood cells. Cobalamin also maintains a healthy myelin sheath which insulates the nerves.

Amongst the causes of deficiency are veganism, pregnancy, old age, alcohol and heavy smoking. Unfortunately, vitamin B_{12} is confined to foods of animal origin, apart from nutritional yeast and fermented foods. There are no reported symptoms of excessive intake of this vitamin.

Cobalamin has been used therapeutically in the treatment of pernicious anaemia, moodiness, poor memory, mental confusion and tiredness. It also acts as an appetite stimulant.

FOLIC ACID   Folic acid is needed in the formation of blood cells and the production of genetic material. It is also necessary for growth, healthy nervous and digestive systems, and transmitting hereditary characteristics. Folic acid is known as the anti-anaemia vitamin because in 1945 it was first demonstrated that it cured anaemia during pregnancy. This vitamin is also useful in the treatment of various mental disorders including psychosis, mental deterioration and schizophrenia. Because of the importance of folic acid in cell division, research is under way to see if the vitamin taken before conception could prevent various congenital diseases of the nervous system, such as spina bifida. The results so far have been promising.

Deficiency in folic acid is common during pregnancy and other groups at risk are the very young and elderly. The contraceptive pill and many other drugs can also be a cause of deficiency. The symptoms include weakness, fatigue, breathlessness, irritability, insomnia and mental confusion. Habitual abortion, possible spina bifida, premature birth and premature separation of the placenta from the uterus have also been reported.

The symptoms of excessive intake include loss of appetite, nausea and sleep disturbances.

The best sources of folic acid are dark green vegetables like broccoli, endive and spinach.

VITAMIN C

Of all the vitamins, vitamin C is probably the best known. It is essential to promote growth in children and to protect against the deficiency disease of scurvy. This vitamin plays an important role in maintaining the health of bones, teeth, gums, cartilage, capillaries and connective tissue. It also acts as a natural antiseptic. Vitamin C controls blood cholesterol levels, maintains healthy sex organs, provides resistance to infections, especially colds and flu, and promotes iron absorption from food by making folic acid active. Anti-stress hormones are also produced by vitamin C and it is an important antioxidant. Recent research suggests that vitamin C may help in preventing gastric and oesophageal cancer. Arthritis, high blood cholesterol levels, bleeding gums, scurvy, anaemia and respiratory diseases have all been treated quite successfully by vitamin C.

Stress and alcohol both inhibit the absorption of vitamin C, as do aspirins, contraceptive pills, antibiotics and anti-arthritic drugs. Athletes, diabetics and anyone undergoing surgery or suffering from accidental wounds require extra amounts of this important vitamin.

Surprisingly, deficiency is widespread, probably because people do not eat enough leafy green vegetables and citrus fruits, relying instead on packeted fruit juices which soon lose their vitamin C content once opened. Deficiency symptoms include weakness, muscle and joint pain, gingivitis, bleeding gums, loosening of teeth and irritability.

Symptoms of excessive intake are nausea, abdominal cramps and diarrhoea. However, overdose is rare and it is widely regarded as a safe vitamin.

Good sources of vitamin C are:

FRUITS		VEGETABLES	
blackberries	melons	beetroot	courgettes
blackcurrants	oranges	broccoli	green or red
cranberries	passion fruit	Brussels	peppers
grapefruit	pineapples	sprouts	lettuce
Kiwi fruit	raspberries	cabbage	mustard and
lemons	strawberries	carrots	cress
limes		cauliflower	onions
			parsley
			tomatoes
			watercress

Mineral Matters

Minerals perform important functions in our bodies and yet they have only recently had the spotlight focused upon them. In the past vitamins have stolen the limelight.

You need to ingest minerals from your diet as the body itself cannot manufacture them. The most efficient way is by eating a lot of fruit and vegetables, whole but especially in the form of juices.

Nutritionally speaking, minerals are split into two groups: macro elements and trace elements, depending on how much of a particular mineral we require. If our bodies require a mineral in quantities in excess of 100 milligrams every day, then it is classed as a macro element. Minerals that we require in smaller quantities are in the trace element group. Both groups are essential. Macro elements are important in the transmission of nerve impulses, whilst trace elements are important in the formation of hormones and enzymes by the body.

Recent research programmes show mineral deficiency to be fairly widespread in western populations. Calcium, iron and zinc are the minerals which appear most often to be deficient. In this country, one in four children has an iron deficiency – they are anaemic.

The remaining part of this chapter looks at the essential minerals your body requires. You need never be deficient in any of them if you juice fruit and vegetables on a regular basis.

CALCIUM

Calcium is one of the most important minerals and is especially crucial for growing children and females. Bones are hardened during growth with calcium absorbed from food. Calcium is also necessary for tooth formation and for the normal activity of nerves and muscles. A good regular intake of calcium is particularly important for children as a deficiency in this mineral may not only stunt growth, but may increase the risk of oesteoporosis developing in middle age. Women are especially at risk from this. Although bone formation stops in adulthood, calcium is constantly required because it is withdrawn from the skeleton and replaced at an equal rate when you are in good heath. Consequently, enough calcium must always be taken in. Calcium also helps to control blood cholesterol levels and aids blood clotting. The absorption of calcium is greatly helped by vitamin D. So get out in that sunlight!

Excess intake of calcium is not thought to be harmful as the body will reject and excrete any unnecessary amounts into the urine, faeces and sweat. Some people, though very few in number, may absorb abnormally high levels of calcium from their food, a disease called idiopathic hypercalcuria, which can result in desposits of calcium being formed in the kidneys, commonly called kidney stones.

A deficiency in this mineral will result in symptoms of rickets in children and in adults osteoporosis, bone pain and slow healing of fractures. Muscle weakness, twitches and spasms may also be experienced.

Causes of deficiency include low dietary intake, vitamin D shortage, the contraceptive pill, pregnancy, breast feeding and increased intake of uncooked bran, phosphates, oxalic acid and animal fats.

Good sources of calcium are broccoli, kale, parsley and watercress.

COPPER

Copper is an essential trace element for man and is needed for blood formation, where it helps in the absorption of iron and its incorporation into haemoglobin. This mineral is also required in the formation of healthy bones, in developing resistance to infection and is also partially responsible for the natural colouring pigments that form skin and hair.

Adults are unlikely to suffer from copper deficiency as most foods contain small amounts of the mineral and much of the copper we receive doesn't originate in the food we eat anyway. The processing and storage of food, pesticides and fungicides, copper containers such as kettles, pans and water pipes, all supply us with copper in minute but sufficient amounts.

However, should a deficiency arise, the symptoms include anaemia, irritability, water retention, brittle bones and the depigmentation of the hair in adults. In children deficiency would result in failure to thrive, diarrhoea, pale skin and depigmentation of the hair.

Like other trace elements, copper is toxic in excess and too much would cause diarrhoea, nausea and vomiting in the short term. In the long term an accumulation in the liver would result in liver damage. It would be almost impossible to overdose on copper from fruit and vegetable juices. It would be advisable, however, to avoid using unlined copper pans.

Good sources of copper are found in green vegetables.

IODINE

An essential trace element that is crucial for efficient thyroid functioning which determines the level of metabolism in the body. As a natural antiseptic, iodine is useful in helping to rid blocked mucous passages. Fruit and vegetables contain varying amounts of this trace element, depending on the soil's iodine content, which differs from place to place. In western countries deficiency is extremely unlikely. The classic deficiency disease is called goitre in adults, and cretinism in children. Excess intake is also extremely unlikely.

FACT FILE

The Midlands and South West England have soil so lacking in iodine that the common occurrence of goitre became known as 'Derbyshire Neck'

Radishes are a particularly good source of iodine but fruit and vegetables generally will contain some iodine, depending on the soil content of the trace element.

IRON

Everyone needs adequate amounts of this mineral but care and attention should be taken during pregnancy. Women and children are particularly likely to develop anaemia. Certain circumstances could also require the body to need more iron. For example, after surgery or an accident and during convalescence an iron-rich diet is beneficial. Iron is vital for the formation of red blood cells, which then carry oxygen to every cell in the body. It is also a useful mineral in developing resistance to infection and keeping up our energy levels too. In fact, it affects virtually our whole well being, both mental and physical.

FACT FILE

About 10 per cent of women in the affluent west are thought to be deficient in iron

---

Iron deficiency is fairly common, causing anaemia which is characterized by tiredness, lack of stamina, breathlessness, headaches, insomnia, palpitations and skin pallor. In some cases instability and mental lethargy can also occur.

Most people simply reject excess intakes of iron by excreting it, so overdosing isn't really a problem.

The iron in vegetables such as spinach is poorly absorbed, and so increasing your vitamin C intake is useful to aid the process

---

Good sources of iron are green vegetables. Parsley is especially rich in iron.

MAGNESIUM

Magnesium is an important mineral that performs many fundamental roles in the body and is present in almost every cell. This mineral is therefore vital in maintaining the structure of cells and their replication as well as transmitting nerve impulses and muscle movement. Magnesium aids the absorption of two other important minerals, calcium and potassium, both of which help to promote strong bones. It is also necessary for converting calories into energy.

Magnesium has been found to be of benefit in treating a number of ailments and diseases such as pre-menstrual tension, morning sickness, arteriosclerosis, angina, abnormal heartbeats, insomnia and kidney stones. It is generally thought that chronic heart diseases may be related to low levels of magnesium in the body because the heart muscle of those dying from heart attacks has lower than normal levels of magnesium present. Death rates from this cause are much higher in soft-water areas throughout the world, and magnesium is the missing mineral in soft water.

Magnesium deficiency can occur in certain groups of people even though the mineral is widespread in food. The elderly, heavy drinkers, athletes, pregnant women, dieters, diabetics and those people taking diuretics and the contraceptive pill are most at risk. Deficiency symptoms include tiredness, weakness, nervousness, palpitations, muscle cramps and hyperactivity in children.

Excessive intake of magnesium is highly unlikely to have any effect as normal individuals will reject the excess into their intestines. Those with kidney disease may experience flushing of the skin, thirst, low blood pressure and shallow breathing.

Good sources of magnesium are found in leafy green vegetables.

Manganese

Manganese is a trace element which is thought to be essential for humans. Research into this nutrient has been fairly limited, but what research there is indicates that it is important for growing and maintaining a sound nervous system, developing and maintaining healthy bones, reproductive health and metabolism. Because it is an antioxidant it seeks out and fights free radicals in the body and maintains cell vitality.

It is extremely unlikely that you will absorb an excess of this trace element from oral ingestion and there are no specific deficiency symptoms associated with manganese.

Good sources are beet greens, broccoli, Brussels sprouts, cabbage, carrots, ginger-root and spinach.

Phosphorus

Phosphorus is an important mineral and is a constituent of cells, a structural component of teeth and bones and it is required for healthy strong nails, hair and cuticles. This mineral plays a powerful role in the production of energy and is useful in countering fatigue.

All foods, with the exception of sugar, spirits and fats, contain some phosphorus. In fact, excess intake of this mineral could be easily achieved from consuming soft drinks, processed and junk foods as manufacturers use it widely. Overdose can cause diarrhoea and prevent the absorption of other minerals such as iron, calcium, magnesium and zinc.

Deficiency of phosphorus is unlikely as the mineral is so widespread in a variety of foods. Symptoms of deficiency include loss of appetite, weakness, bone pain, irritability and speech disorders.

Good sources of phosphorus are carrots, cauliflower, parsley, apples, grapefruit, oranges, pears and pineapples.

Potassium

Nearly all food contains potassium and fruit and vegetables are rich sources. This mineral is needed to keep a normal fluid balance in cells, to maintain the acid/alkali balance of the blood and for the functioning of the nervous system. The body possesses a balance of potassium and sodium which is important to maintain. Unfortunately, many people have a high salt intake, the main source of sodium, and they do not increase their potassium intake accordingly. Juicing is an efficient way of doing this. The other thing to do to keep the balance would be to reduce the sodium intake.

This potassium-sodium balance is crucial as it stimulates and regulates the heartbeat and appears to be strongly associated with controlling high blood pressure and strokes. Potassium also tightens the collagen in the skin tissues, making it appear smoother, healthier and younger looking.

Potassium deficiency is rare in healthy adults and children, but when there are increased losses from the body, say during bouts of diarrhoea, vomiting, kidney diseases or the use of diuretics, it can occur. The elderly are at risk because they eat less potassium than average in their diet. The symptoms of deficiency are muscle weakness, loss of appetite, drowsiness, vomiting, mental confusion and, in severe cases, heart attacks.

A high potassium diet is not thought to be harmful as the excess is eliminated in a healthy person by the kidneys. Those suffering with a kidney disease could accumulate high levels of potassium in the bloodstream which could possibly cause a heart attack.

Good sources of potassium are:

FRUIT		VEGETABLES	
blackberries	passion fruit	asparagus	mustard and
blackcurrants	peaches	beetroot	cress
cherries	pineapple	Brussels	parsley
grapefruit	plums	sprouts	parsnips
grapes	pomegranates	celery	peppers
Kiwi fruit	strawberries	courgettes	potatoes
nectarines		leeks	spinach
		lettuce	tomatoes
			watercress

SELENIUM

Research into this important trace element has mushroomed in recent years and it is increasingly being seen as an effective guard against our two major killers – cancer and heart disease. No wonder there is a lot of interest in selenium. And it doesn't end there, for it is also useful in reducing the painful inflammation caused by arthritis, for treating high blood pressure and for fertility. It helps us stay younger looking because it makes our skin more elastic and wrinkle-free, our hair shiny and strong, and our eyes bright and clear. It is a very effective antioxidant. As if all this weren't enough, it also maintains our resistance to disease and promotes the male sexual reproductive capacity in the production of hormones. What a mineral!

Plants absorb selenium from the soil and so it is the content of the soil that determines the content of selenium in the local diet, and there are wide variations between regions. Selenium deficiency can occur if your diet is high in refined and processed foods, but also if you consume food mainly grown in selenium deficient soil. Heart disease, cancer and muscular disease are symptomatic of selenium deficiency.

Selenium is toxic if taken in excess, and symptoms include dental caries in children, hair loss, abnormal nails and skin depigmentation in adults.

Good sources of selenium are asparagus, broccoli, cabbage and garlic.

SILICON

This trace element is probably the wonder nutrient for keeping a youthful appearance. All the connective tissue of the body contains silicon. It is an important element in cartilage where it plays a crucial role in the strength and elasticity of gristle. Artery walls, an important feature of blood pressure control, are kept elastic by silicon.

By increasing your silicon intake you will do miraculous things for your looks. Your skin will be unblemished, unwrinkled, elastic, firm and smooth. Nails will grow stronger, and your hair will improve, becoming stronger and thicker. It may also deter premature greying.

Any toxic effects of silicon are confined to inhalation of silica, not from dietary sources; and deficiency is highly unlikely as it is so widespread in our fruit and vegetables.

Good sources of silicon are apricots, cherries, all green vegetables, cucumbers, green peppers and lettuce.

Sodium

Most of us consume far too much sodium in the form of salt and this gives us most of our sodium intake. This type of inorganic sodium chloride causes health problems. The sodium consumed from fruit and vegetable juices is organic and natural and our bodies can absorb sufficient of the mineral for their needs without having to sprinkle salt over everything we eat.

Sodium is important to maintain the sodium–potassium balance in the body, for it keeps us functioning efficiently, aids digestion and maintains the heart rate at normal levels. It is very useful for fighting fatigue.

Dietary-related sodium deficiency is extremely unlikely, but it can occur with dehydration, for example, in very high temperatures. The result would be dryness in the mouth, mental apathy and a loss of appetite.

An excess intake of sodium leads to increased urination and in a healthy individual the kidneys have no difficulty in coping, as long as there is a sufficient intake of water. The situation resulting from long-term excess is different, as high sodium levels are strongly associated with major diseases such as heart disease, cancer, high blood pressure and strokes.

Good fruit and vegetable sources of sodium are pineapples, strawberries, carrots, celery, radishes and tomatoes.

Sulphur

Sulphur is a constitutent of all proteins and as such is an essential element for man. Sulphur occurs mainly in the nails, skin, joints and hair. Therefore it contributes greatly to health and beauty. In fact, whether or not you have curly hair depends on how much sulphur it contains. Five per cent of the total weight of sheep's wool, which is very curly, is sulphur.

Nearly all dietary sulphur is derived from protein and there is no evidence of deficiency states in either man or animals.

FACT FILE

The characteristic smell of burning hair is due to its high sulphur content

---

Sulphur is important for the metabolism of the liver and for keeping our intestinal walls healthy.

Good sources of sulphur are cabbage, garlic, kale and onions.

ZINC

Zinc is an essential trace element for humans, animals and plants, playing many important roles in the body. It is necessary for growth, sexual maturity, wound healing and the senses of taste and smell. Probably its most important function is in protecting the immune system. The highest concentrations of zinc in the body are found in the prostate and in semen and sperm. Consequently, it has been found that this trace element is useful in treating impotency in men, infertility problems and preventing and treating prostate conditions. Skin ailments such as eczema, psoriasis, rosacea and acne have also benefited from zinc consumption.

Zinc deficiency gives rise to lack of physical, mental and sexual development. It also causes growth failure, loss of the sense of taste and smell, poor appetite, a susceptibility to infections and smelly feet!

Alcohol, fever and artificial kidney machine treatment are some of the factors which can inhibit zinc absorption. After surgery or burns there can also be zinc malabsorption.

FACT FILE

When zinc is lacking in hair, its growth slows down considerably and can even stop

---

Excess intake of zinc from dietary sources is unlikely as the excess is excreted in urine and sweat. But very large doses, orally in supplements or by contamination, are toxic and cause vomiting.

Good sources are broccoli, Brussels sprouts, cabbage, carrots, cauliflower, ginger-root, kale, kohlrabi, leafy green vegetables, parsley, spinach and watercress.

CHAPTER THREE

FEELING FRUITY

I find it exhilarating to wander amongst fruit stalls because the variety that is available to us is astounding. We are spoilt for choice and it's such good fun experimenting with unfamiliar, weird and wonderful delights, as well as the common old apples and pears. I'm not fit to be let loose around fruit stalls – it always costs me an absolute fortune because I just can't resist anything that looks appetizing or different.

FACT FILE

Fresh fruits are 80–90 per cent water, making them excellent for flushing out the system

---

What I do try to look for is organic fruit, but it is difficult to find in my part of the world. Most of the time I have to buy produce that has been treated with various chemicals – herbicides and pesticides – that are potentially harmful to life. Another nice thing about organic fruit is that it is like going back in time to when fruits had very specific seasons. You buy particular fruits and varieties at certain times of year. You can't store them indefinitely or lengthen their growing season artificially. So you can find unusual varieties, some-times local ones, of apples and pears that you don't find in mass-cultivated produce. And the flavour of organic fruit is far superior. But do remember organic produce will not keep as long as chemical laden ones, certainly won't look as attractive, and may have the occasional unwelcome lodger in the form of worms. So keep a look out!

Washing fruit with a gentle biodegradable cleanser (available from health shops and some supermarkets) is essential if the fruit is not organic. Very often chemicals and pesticides are sprayed on to the fruit and this needs to be removed by either washing or peeling. Do make sure you rinse the fruit well under cold running water and dry it thoroughly before storing.

This chapter looks at various fruits which are particularly useful in maintaining our health and beauty. The list is not exhaustive but it does cover most of the popular fruits and one or two with which you may be unfamiliar. All are easily available from your supermarket or street market. They are all delicious. The major nutrients and the particular benefits of each fruit is given, as well as what to look for when you buy them, how to store them and how to juice them.

Juicing fruit is fun and home juicing bears no resemblance at all to those processed cartons that sit on supermarket shelves, either in taste or nutritional content. Be adventurous and experiment with the whole array of fruits at your disposal; mix and match flavours and nutrients to make your own designer juice. Get the whole family involved – it's great fun!

FACT FILE

Although fruit contains acids it does not increase the acidity of the body – even for people with digestive problems

---

Please remember that fruits, and therefore fruit juices, have a very high sugar content, albeit natural sugar. People suffering from any kind of blood sugar problem, or on a low sugar diet, should limit their intake of fruit juices. If you are in any doubt at all, please consult your doctor or dietician.

APPLES

Apples are the most popular fruit in Britain, accounting for approximately one-third of all the fresh fruit purchased. The benefits and health-giving qualities of this fruit have been known for centuries throughout many civilizations. I was always told as a child by my mum that 'An apple a day keeps the doctor away' – not to mention the dentist! That maxim has stood me in good stead throughout my life.

There are many varieties of apples available to us these days, all with very different flavours. My particular favourites are Beauty of Bath, Cox's Orange Pippins, Gala, Granny Smith, McIntosh Reds, Red Delicious and Russets. Luckily, at least a couple of these apple varieties are available at any one time of the year and all are excellent for juicing. But try your own favourites.

I firmly believe that it is better to buy organically grown apples in preference to those treated with chemicals. Don't be lured by the bright shiny apples often found in supermarkets – they have been waxed to preserve them still further. Apples should always be peeled before juicing or eating if they are not organic, as many of the chemicals and waxes used are often not removed by washing. I find that organic apples tend to have a better flavour, though you should watch out for the odd worm present in the fruit. They may be quite nutritious, but I don't think you would want to juice and drink one!

FACT FILE

Apples and pears are likely to contain antioxidants to prevent browning of the flesh during storage

---

Apples are high in pectin, which is good news, for it keeps the bowel active, removes toxins from the intestines and, along with the vitamin C present, lowers cholesterol levels. The relatively high levels of potassium and phosphorus help digestive problems and flush the kidneys. In fact, a very good friend of mine recommends eating apples prior to a journey, especially on the sea, to prevent travel sickness. Apples are also great detoxifiers and will benefit anyone who suffers from arthritis, rheumatism or gout.

Buying and Storing

The apples you buy, especially for juicing, should be crisp and firm, and show no signs of soft spots or blemishes. Wash the apples and dry them very well before placing them in the crisp container of the refrigerator until required.

While many people realize that good flavour is often found in the less brightly coloured fruits, good colour will remain a lure to us all.

But don't let this stop you trying the less attractive apples. My absolute favourite is the Russet which is dull and dowdy to look at but its flavour is wonderful.

APRICOTS

Apricots go back a long way, probably as far back as 2200 BC in China and by AD 50 they were being enjoyed in Italy as a gourmet food. It took until the fifteenth century for these bright yellow orbs to be widespread in Europe. Apricots are packed full of vitamin A, due to their high content of beta-carotene, which is important in fighting cancer. The more brightly coloured the fruit, the more beta-carotene it will contain. They are also a good source of potassium and magnesium – excellent for stamina and energy. Silicon can be found in these little fruits which is beneficial to the skin, hair and nails. Apricots also contain iron, crucial for our blood.

Buying and Storing

Only firmish, brightly coloured, goldy, pinky fruits should be bought, as this means they are sweet. Wash and dry the fruit and store it in the crisp container of the refrigerator. Remove the stone prior to juicing. Again, it is worth trying to get organic apricots.

BANANAS

Bananas are not ideal for juicing because they contain about twice as much carbohydrate as other fruit, and clog the machine up! They were first cultivated in India 5000 years ago. Because of their high potassium content they are particularly beneficial for the heart. In fact, a few years ago, 'The Banana Diet' become popular in the United States for heart patients for this very reason. Zinc, iron, folic acid, calcium and vitamin B6 are also supplied in good amounts by this fruit.

Buying and Storing

Green bananas should not be eaten as they could cause indigestion. Look for under-ripe bananas that will ripen if left at room temperature for a couple of days.

BLACKBERRIES

Blackberries are native to Britain and Europe and are a rich source of vitamins C and E. Wild blackberries contain more vitamin E than the cultivated variety and have the benefit of being organic, not to mention free. However, I avoid picking them from busy roadsides because they tend to be rather dusty and will have absorbed exhaust fumes. You will find them in the autumn in most areas of the country.

Potassium, calcium, magnesium, beta-carotene and some of the B complex vitamins are all present in blackberries, so they are beneficial for heart disease, cancer, strokes, high blood pressure and pre-menstrual tension. They are also good for your eyesight and skin.

Buying and Storing

Plump, luscious looking fruit which is a uniformly dark colour of purple/black is the best. The fruit should come away from the stalk quite easily. Red ones are not ripe, will not yield much juice and certainly won't taste at all sweet. They should be washed and left to drain on absorbent paper before being stored in the refrigerator. If not dried completely, mould will quickly develop. Consume as soon as possible.

BLACKCURRANTS

Blackcurrants are extremely rich in vitamin C, containing between 150 and 230 milligrams per 100 grams when fresh. They are also a useful source of potassium, calcium, magnesium, beta-carotene and some of the B complex vitamins. They are especially useful in fighting heart disease and cancer. They really have a beautiful flavour and are extremely good to juice. Mostly available in autumn.

Buying and Storing

You should look for firm but not hard blackcurrants, with a deep purple to black colour. Again the red ones are not fully ripened and should not be used as they will be bitter in flavour, and not very juicy. After washing they should be left to drain before being stored in the refrigerator. Blackcurrants should be consumed as soon as possible.

CHERRIES

Cherries are first thought to have been cultivated in the Near East, namely Mesopotamia, and their appearance in Europe is relatively recent. I love cherries and they give a wonderful flavour when juiced. Cherries are packed with vitamins and minerals – particularly high in iron, potassium, magnesium, silicon and beta-carotene.

Buying and Storing

Cherries do not ripen once they have been picked. You need to choose cherries that are plump and ripe – not too soft and not too hard. Wash and dry. Ideally they should be kept in a refrigerator until required. Remember to remove the stones before juicing!

CITRUS FRUITS

The peel of citrus fruits is likely to contain various preservatives to prevent mould, so they should be washed thoroughly. You may even consider peeling the fruit – I tend to.

The term 'citrus fruits' covers a wide range and includes grapefruit, lemons, limes, oranges and tangerines. All citrus fruits are very useful sources of vitamin C, but in order to gain maximum benefit, you need to drink the juice almost immediately because the vitamin dissipates rapidly. Citrus fruits also contain beta-carotene in useful amounts.

When you juice citrus fruits, you can put the pips and membrane into the juicer, but avoid adding the peel of grapefruit, oranges and tangerines, as it is difficult to digest. Peel these fruits prior to juicing. You may find that your juicing machine will not work properly if the peel is not removed from all citrus fruits. Check your instruction booklet if in any doubt.

Once picked from the tree, citrus fruits do not ripen further, so bear that in mind when you buy them.

GRAPEFRUIT

I prefer the sweeter type of grapefruit such as the ruby and pink varieties. It is a marvellous fruit to juice on its own. Grapefruit is a good source of vitamin C, phosphorus, calcium and potassium. It is beneficial in preventing bleeding gums and combating colds and flu. High levels of pectin are present, which is good for those suffering from circulatory or digestive problems. Bioflavonoids are also contained in grapefruit which protect vitamin C, are anti-inflammatory, and protect the blood vessels. Both pectin and bioflavonoids are found in the white pith and the membrane of the fruit.

Buying and Storing

The best juicy grapefruit are those which have smooth, thin skins and feel heavy for their size. They should feel slightly springy to the touch. Store grapefruit in the refrigerator.

LEMONS

Lemons are extremely useful in juicing for they possess a lot of valuable nutrients and add a nice tang which is thirst quenching. Lemons are rich in bioflavonoids and pectin. Lemons have a very high vitamin C content, twice as much as oranges, in fact, and also contain the B vitamins. Traditionally lemons have always been used to cure colds and flu.

Buying and Storing

As with grapefruit, look for smooth, thin-skinned ones that feel heavy for their size. Avoid lemons with any green on their skin, as they will be more acidic than usual. Wash and dry before storing in the refrigerator.

LIMES

Limes give a nice flavour to any juice to which they are added. They contain less vitamin C than lemons but are still a rich source. Bioflavonoids, pectin and potassium are all found in limes. British seamen were nicknamed 'Limeys' because they were given this fruit on long sea voyages to prevent scurvy. Unfortunately, because they have a lower vitamin C content than lemons, outbreaks of scurvy reappeared and so lemons were reissued.

Buying and Storing

Rough, dimple-skinned fruit means that the lime is dry and not full of flavour. Buy smooth, thin-skinned fruits. Wash, dry and keep in a cool place – the refrigerator is too cold for limes.

ORANGES

Oranges were introduced into Europe about 2000 years ago. They are thought to have originated in China and South East Asia. Juiced oranges are great, creating a thick foamy drink. The orange is rich in vitamin C, B complex vitamins, beta-carotene, bioflavonoids, pectin, potassium, zinc and phosphorus. Orange juice protects against colds, flu, heart disease and strokes, and will strengthen blood vessels and capillaries.

Buying and Storing

As with other citrus fruits, choose thin-skinned, smooth oranges. Store them in the refrigerator and eat within five days of purchase.

TANGERINES

Another name for this fruit is the mandarin orange, denoting its origins in the Far East. Tangerines didn't appear in Europe until the eighteenth century. These loose-skinned fruits are jam-packed full of nutrients and one small tangerine has more vitamin C than some large oranges. They are also a good source of vitamin B and beta-carotene. As with other citrus fruits, they are useful in warding off colds and flu, and also contain pectin and bioflavonoids.

Buying and Storing

Buy tangerines with bright skins and a heavy feel for their size. Avoid bruised fruit. Tangerines should be kept in a refrigerator. Eat within five days of purchase. You can find tangerines in the shops during the wintertime, especially around Christmas.

CRANBERRIES

Cranberries are native to Europe and the British Isles. The American cranberry is larger than our varieties. It is a fruit which contains quinine, vitamin C, iron, potassium and beta-carotene. Because of the quinine, the taste is quite bitter and it is best to combine the cranberry with sweeter fruits such as pears, grapes or apples. The quinine helps to maintain the health of the bladder, kidneys and prostate, and assists in the prevention of cancer of the prostate. Cranberries have been found to be beneficial in treating a variety of urinary tract infections such as cystitis and they are being used increasingly to treat kidney stones. They are also helpful in preventing and fighting colds and flu and so they make a particularly useful winter juice.

Unfortunately, these small dark red berries only have a short season, November and December, and so it is useful to freeze some for future use. Luckily they do freeze very well. You can use them, thawed, for juicing with no loss of nutrients.

Buying and Storing

Choose plump, firm, red berries and avoid small, hard, wrinkled ones which will not have a lot of juice. They should be washed, dried and stored in the refrigerator.

GRAPES

Grapes have one of the highest sugar contents of all fruits, which makes them very useful for adding to other, less sweet fruits and vegetables. Grapes give juices a delicious flavour.

The grapevine is one of the oldest cultivated plants, dating back at least 6000 years. The plant is thought to have its origins in Western Asia. There is little nutritional difference between black and white grapes, and they both contain potassium, though the black ones have slightly more. Potassium is an important mineral which regulates and stimulates the heartbeat and maintains the acid/alkali balance of the blood, not to mention reducing the risk of high blood pressure, heart disease and strokes. Iron is also found in grapes and this is crucial for red blood cell formation and maintaining our overall

34

physical and mental health. Grapes stimulate digestive juices and so are useful in treating problems of the digestive system. They also keep the bowel active and soothe our nerves. Grapes are also excellent at fighting fatigue and for ailments such as gout, rheumatism and arthritis as they help to eliminate waste from the system.

Because grapes have such a high sugar content, it is advisable for people with any blood sugar problem to avoid them.

Buying and Storing

I try to buy organically-grown grapes, but it is quite difficult to find them in the shops. Look out for grapes that look fresh and plump – not old wizened ones that are dropping off their stems. 'White' grapes should be slightly yellowish in colour, whilst 'black' ones should be rich and dark all over. The stems should be green and fresh. Old looking brown stems are a dead give away that the grapes are not fresh. Fortunately, grapes are available all year round. The unfortunate thing is that they are probably more chemically treated than any other fruit. Always wash grapes well, dry them thoroughly and store in the refrigerator. There's no need to buy seedless or to de-seed before juicing.

KIWI FRUIT

The original name for this fruit was 'Chinese gooseberry', then New Zealand aggressively marketed it and it became known as 'Kiwi'. New Zealand is now the major exporter of this delicious green fruit but it also comes from America. As an import Kiwis are available all year round.

Kiwi fruit is a rich source of vitamin C and, in fact, contains twice as much as oranges! The fruit juices very well and gives a good flavour. Kiwi fruit has an unfortunate appearance in that it is a small, oval, hairy brown object – not in the least bit attractive. However, this situation changes once you cut it open to reveal the most beautiful deep green flesh speckled with black, shiny edible seeds. All you then have to do is wash the fruit and juice it – what could be simpler?

Buying and Storing

Kiwi fruit should be firm, but not hard; it should give way under pressure. Keep Kiwi fruit in the refrigerator until required.

MANGOES

The mango is a beautifully fragrant and well-flavoured fruit that is more popular in tropical countries, especially India, than in the western world. But this situation is changing as it becomes more widely available and can be bought throughout the year.

Mangoes are a good source of vitamin C and the ripe, orange coloured fruit also contains beta-carotene, although far less is found in the unripe ones. Potassium and some of the B complex vitamins are also present in this wonderful fruit.

Mangoes should be peeled before juicing. Don't forget to remove the large oval stone inside the fruit.

Buying and Storing

Mangoes have smooth skins and can be a variety of colours, from greens and yellows to reds and oranges. I personally prefer the red/orange ones as they tend to be sweeter, more perfumed and juicier. The mango should be fairly firm, but yield to pressure when squeezed gently. Avoid bruised and very soft fruit. Store at room temperature.

MELONS

The melon species has many varieties which look and taste very different. The one thing they all have in common is their high water content – 94 per cent to be precise. They are therefore wonderfully low in calories and ideal for juicing. 'Winter melons' such as the honeydew and the dark green skinned melons have whitish or green flesh which contains little beta-carotene. But the orange-fleshed Ogen and Cantaloup are a very good source of this vitamin. The watermelon is the exception as it contains less vitamin C, beta-carotene and potassium than other varieties.

Melons are excellent for people suffering from kidney problems because of their diuretic properties. They are also a good tonic as they help to cleanse the body of waste.

If you can buy organic melons, and if your juicer can stand it, do not remove the rind prior to juicing – juice the whole lot. Remember to wash it first! Otherwise it is better to peel the fruit. Watermelon rind is a rich source of potassium and beta-carotene, whilst the white inner rind provides us with zinc, iodine, more potassium and a variety of enzymes that aid digestion. Luckily some variety of melon is available all the year round and we increasingly see different types in our shops with which we can experiment.

Buying and Storing

Cantaloup melons should smell sweet and have tiny crevices around the stem end. They should yield under gentle pressure. These melons will ripen at room temperature, otherwise keep them in a refrigerator.

Honeydew melons should also yield under gentle pressure, especially at the stem end. Avoid hard fruits as they are not ripe, their flesh is likely to taste like turnip, and they yield little juice. If they are ripe, store them in the refrigerator, otherwise they can be left at room temperature.

Watermelons can be tested for ripeness by listening to them. If you flick them with your fingers and they make a hollow sound they are ready to be eaten and will be full of juice and sweetness. The green skin should be dull and not shiny. They are best left at room temperature until they have been cut open, after which they should be placed in the refrigerator.

FACT FILE

As fruits ripen their acid content falls

NECTARINES

See peaches, p. 38.

Papaya

Sometimes called pawpaw , this fruit is native to tropical America. It is a good source of vitamin C, beta-carotene, B complex vitamins and potassium. Recent research indicates that the enzyme papain contained in this fruit aids the digestion of proteins.

Papaya look like rounded pears that are green and yellow in colour. When they are cut open the flesh is pinky, peachy with black edible seeds. Papaya is good for juicing, but peel the fruit first. Papaya is available for much of the year.

Buying and Storing

Ripeness is shown by a speckling of yellow on the green skin. The fruit should feel firm and yet yield to gentle pressure. Avoid bruised or wrinkled fruit. Keep unripe fruit at room temperature, and ripe fruit in the refrigerator.

Passion Fruit

Probably the most ugly of all fruits: wrinkled, black and the size of an egg. It possesses a unique flavour, very fragrant and perfumed, which transforms any juice into a distinctly different drink. Once cut open, the yellowy transparent flesh is inseparable from the edible black seeds. The fruit is a good source of potassium, magnesium and vitamin C. Remove the flesh and seeds from the hard wrinkled skin before juicing. Passion fruit is available most of the year.

Buying and Storing

Choose passion fruit with deep wrinkles in the hard skin as this shows the flesh will be juicy, sweet and full of flavour. Avoid smooth-skinned fruit. Store at room temperature.

Peaches

Peaches are delectable little fruits which originated in China and were introduced into Britain in the sixteenth century. Their beautiful flavour when juiced makes them nice mixers. Try it with Kiwi or strawberry juice. Please remember to remove the stone before juicing. This fruit is a good source of beta-carotene, the B complex vitamins and the mineral potassium. Drinking peach juice will improve your skin and eyesight, help protect against cancer, heart disease, strokes and high blood pressure. Unfortunately they are only widely available in the summer months.

Buying and Storing

Choose peaches that are not blemished. They should feel fairly firm but not like rocks. Hard peaches are not ripe and will yield only a little juice. I find that the rosier the colour of the peach the sweeter it tends to be. Wash, dry and keep in the refrigerator until required.

PEARS

Pears are native to Europe, especially southern parts. The varieties we are used to seeing today were developed in the eighteenth century in France and Belgium, with the 'Conference Pear' popular in Britain. Pears of one variety or another are available all the year round. They all have one thing in common and that is their sweetness. This concentrated sweetness makes them ideal for mixing with other juices, especially vegetables and less sweet fruits.

Pears are great for the cardiovascular system, as they contain plenty of the vitamins B_1, B_2, B_3 and folic acid. These are the important B complex vitamins that are useful in boosting energy levels. Vitamin C, phosphorus, potassium and calcium are also present in the humble pear.

Pears are good for relieving constipation and in treating digestive problems because of their high levels of pectin.

Buying and Storing

Always buy firm but ripe pears for juicing – soft ones will clog up your juicer! Wash them well, dry and keep in the refrigerator.

PINEAPPLES

The pineapple is a most refreshing fruit that makes your lips pucker on the first taste. Pineapple contains the enzyme bromelain which breaks down proteins and as a consequence is often recommended as an aid to digestion. This fruit is a wonderful, tasty source of many nutrients such as beta-carotene, B complex vitamins and vitamin C.

The minerals chlorine, sodium, potassium, phosphorus, sulphur, calcium, iron and iodine are all found in good supply.

Unless you can find organic pineapples, it is better to peel them before juicing. I haven't found an organic pineapple yet! But you can leave the core in place. Simply slice the pineapple into 25 cm/1 in rounds and then cut it into strips ready for juicing.

Buying and Storing

Pineapples should feel heavy for their size, be a dark golden colour and have a strong, sweet aroma indicating ripeness and sweetness. The juiciest pineapples are the larger plump ones. The real test is whether you can pull a leaf off its stem easily – if you can then it's ripe. But remember that they do not ripen after picking. Keep them at room temperature until cut open, when they should be stored in the refrigerator. Pineapples can be bought throughout the year.

FACT FILE

Fruits are great energy boosters and cleansers of the body

RASPBERRIES

I love raspberries because their flavour is so fresh and clean. I particularly like them with peach juice. It is so full of flavour. It is also very moreish, so be warned!

Raspberries contain significant amounts of vitamin C and various minerals, including potassium, calcium and magnesium. They are also good sources of beta-carotene and contain some of the B complex vitamins. Raspberries are invaluable therefore to those suffering from heart problems, fatigue or depression. These little red fruits are natural astringents and help diseased gums, upset stomachs and bowel problems.

Buying and Storing

Choose raspberries that are plump and deep red in colour. They should be firm with no brown evident on them. Wash and leave to drain on absorbent paper before storing in the refrigerator. Freeze or use as soon as possible after purchase. Raspberries are available during the summer months; or you can use shop-bought frozen brands.

STRAWBERRIES

Strawberries are derived from two American varieties which were introduced into Europe in 1600 and 1800. They are probably the most attractive of fruits because of their wonderful bright red colour and their dainty heart-like shape. They are good sources of vitamin C and are high in potassium and iron. Strawberries are useful for fighting off colds and flu, and good for our skin and eyes. They help to guard against cancer, heart disease, strokes and high blood pressure. They have also been recommended as a cure for arthritis, rheumatism and gout and for eliminating kidney stones. Their high iron content makes them beneficial in treating anaemia and fighting fatigue.

When juiced you may find the liquid too thick and so it is a good idea to mix it with other fruits or even mineral water. Whatever you decide, the taste will be terrific – I guarantee it! They are most widely available in the summer months but look out for imports at other times of year, although these may be costly.

Buying and Storing

You must buy the freshest strawberries you can get your hands on. Better still, grow your own or at least pick your own from a fruit farm. The fruit should be a vivid red with a slight shine, and firm, never soft. The green leaves at the top of the strawberry should be bright and fresh and well attached to the fruit. Wash and leave them to dry on absorbent paper before storing in the refrigerator. Use them as soon as possible, as strawberries don't keep very well.

FACT FILE

Freshly picked fruits contain more vitamin C than stored ones because the vitamin level declines after picking

---

CHAPTER FOUR

VEGETABLE MADNESS

The consumption of fresh vegetables plays a vital role in the health of the body. They not only provide fibre but also important vitamins. Vegetables contain an important source of folic acid and riboflavin, two of the B complex vitamins, beta-carotene and vitamin C. The dark green vegetables, such as spinach and watercress, are particularly rich sources of these nutrients. Carrots are renowned for their beta-carotene content. Minerals are also found in good supply in vegetables, especially potassium and many trace elements. Pectin and chlorophyll are also present, which are crucial elements needed by our bodies.

Regular consumption of vegetables has been found to minimize the risk of contracting diseases such as cancer, heart disease, high blood pressure and strokes and to be beneficial in the treatment of many ailments ranging from arthritis to anaemia.

Consuming your vegetables in juice form is far more efficient and effective, for the nutrients are in a concentrated form and are quickly absorbed by the body because they are already liquid. Some of the juices are great on their own, whilst others are better used as mixers. The juices from green, leafy vegetables such as broccoli, spinach and cabbage are too concentrated and should always be mixed with something like carrot or apple juice. The 'green juices' should never account for more than one third of the volume of any juice and your taste buds may require an even more diluted juice.

As with fruit, I try to buy organic where possible but it is quite difficult and more often than not I have to make do with inorganic produce. Wash the chemicals from the vegetables carefully, using a biodegradable cleanser and rinse very well with cold water. Make sure the vegetables are perfectly dry before storing.

This chapter provides useful nutritional and general information on many vegetables used in the recipes. The idea is to swap and change the vegetables until you devise you own favourite juices which suit your particular health and beauty requirements. And remember, vegetables are a low-energy, low-calorie food and as such are invaluable to anyone wanting to lose inches or weight.

Please note that although vegetable juicing is a sure way of improving both health and beauty, there are some people who need to take a little care. Anyone suffering from kidney stones should avoid juices made from vegetables with a high oxalate content, such as spinach and beetroot, as they could exacerbate the condition.

FACT FILE

Always remove any bruised or mouldy parts of fruits and vegetables before juicing

---

ASPARAGUS

Asparagus has a distinctive flavour which is retained when it is juiced. Unfortunately, it tends to be quite expensive and as such is seen as a luxury food. This vegetable contains significant quantities of beta-carotene, vitamins B, C and E, folic acid and potassium. Asparagus is a well-known aphrodisiac in Greece, where its name originates, and Rome and Egypt. It is also used extensively in the Arab nations. It does in fact contain quite significant quantities of vitamin E and folic acid which are associated strongly with sex drive and performance.

Eyesight, skin and hair are improved because of the presence of beta-carotene, which also guards against cancer and fights the ageing process. Asparagus contains a nutrient called aspargine which is important as it stimulates the kidneys, activates the bowel, purifies the blood and acts as a diuretic. This nutrient is destroyed when cooked, so juicing is the ideal way of obtaining it.

Buying and Storing

Asparagus should be bright green in colour, with strong erect firm tips. Don't buy asparagus that looks limp. It should be washed, dried and stored in the refrigerator until required and eaten within a few days of purchase. Asparagus is generally available from August to October; the season for home grown is May and June.

BEETROOT

Beetroot is related to sugar beet and has a high sugar content, as high as that of an apple, in fact. It also contains potassium, calcium, sulphur and chlorine along with a moderate amount of vitamin C and folic acid. The beetroot has been recognized as being good for the blood for many years, as many an old wives' tale confirms. There is usually some truth in them and beetroot does contain iron which is essential for red blood formation.

In Europe and Russia, beetroot is used as a tonic and to build up resistance to infection. For centuries it has been known to aid the digestive system, especially the liver. It also has a long history in the treatment of cancer as it contains anticarcinogenic substances in the red colouring matter. Beetroot increases the cellular take-up of oxygen which prevents cancer and boosts the immune system. Beetroots and their green tops are mineral rich and help to keep the gall bladder, kidneys and liver healthy. The manganese contained in the green tops helps bodily growth, maintains a healthy nervous system and strong bones and is also especially important to the metabolism and reproductive system.

Buying and Storing

Don't buy beetroots that look wrinkled, as they will be dry and tasteless. The beetroots to look for should be uncooked, firm to the touch and have smooth skins. Their green tops should be bright, vibrant and not at all droopy. Smaller beetroots tend to be tastier and juicier. They should be washed, dried and stored in the refrigerator or a cold place. Beetroot is generally available all year round.

FACT FILE

The pulp left over from juicing beetroot can be used to flavour cakes, sauces and soups

---

Broccoli

A cruciferous vegetable which is available all year round and is also relatively inexpensive. Broccoli is extremely rich in nutrients and does wonders for the body when juiced. It is an excellent source of beta-carotene, which, apart from being a cancer fighting vitamin, also benefits the skin, eyes and hair. Broccoli contains an abundance of vitamin C, folic acid, riboflavin, sulphur, selenium, and potassium. The iron contained in broccoli is more easily absorbed than from most other vegetables, partly because of its high vitamin C content. You cannot afford to be without this important vegetable juice.

Buying and Storing

Choose heads that are bright green and have tight tops. Avoid heads that are turning yellow or even worse, brown. The stems should be firm with fresh looking leaves that are not limp or droopy. Broccoli should be well washed, dried and kept in the refrigerator. As it doesn't keep long it should be eaten within four days of purchase.

Brussels Sprouts

Brussels sprouts are the baby members of the cabbage family and provide bags of vitamins and minerals at a very reasonable cost. The little green balls are a good source of vitamin C, folic acid, potassium, calcium and beta-carotene. The particularly high folic acid content means that the humble little sprout is useful for enhancing your sex life! Cancer, heart disease, high blood pressure and strokes are all diseases thought preventable and treatable by the nutrients contained in this little vegetable.

Buying and Storing

Select small, firm and tight Brussels sprouts that are bright green in colour and look vibrant. Avoid yellowing, soft ones with loose leaves – they are old and as such provide less nutrients. Wash, dry and store in a cold place prior to juicing. Brussels sprouts are traditionally associated with the winter months, and are available from August to March.

45

CABBAGE

What a healthy reputation cabbage has and deservedly so, for, in all its varieties, it is packed with nutrients and minerals. Traditionally, raw cabbage juice has been used in the treatment of ulcers very successfully. For centuries the cabbage has had a reputation for protecting us against stress, infection and cardiac problems. Potassium and iron are found in abundance. Cabbage is a good source of chlorophyll, which, along with iron, helps to treat anaemia. Sulphur, selenium and beta-carotene are also present. Selenium and beta-carotene are important in the fight against cancer, heart disease and inflammatory diseases such as arthritis.

These minerals also help to keep us looking young as they have anti-ageing properties. As if that isn't enough, cabbage has also been found useful in the treatment of digestive problems. That terrible sweet smell which fills the whole house when you cook cabbage is caused by the sulphur content. But this nasty side-effect doesn't occur when juicing this nutritious vegetable.

Buying and Storing

The cabbage should be firm and tight, with a vivid colour and not at all yellow. Because the outer leaves are the most nutritious, these should look fresh and healthy, not wilted or limp. Cabbages should be washed, dried and stored in the refrigerator until required. Luckily cabbages of one variety or another are available throughout the year and are relatively cheap.

CARROTS

Carrots are renowned for their high vitamin A content in the form of beta-carotene. Great for general eyesight and especially night-blindness and colour sight. Generally speaking, the darker coloured varieties of carrot will provide more beta-carotene, as will the older rather than young carrots. One hundred grams (3½ oz) of carrots contain at least three times the recommended daily intake of beta-carotene. They also contain good amounts of vitamin C, most of the B complex vitamins, calcium, potassium, sodium, phosphorous and iron.

They are terrific energy boosters as well as protecting us from heart disease, cancer, strokes and high blood pressure. They also help us to excrete excess alcohol from the liver. Carrots have an extremely high antioxidant level – vitamins A, C and E make them essential for anyone suffering atherosclerosis. Carrot juice protects you against excess ultra-violet rays or radiation, so drink lots of it when you go out into the sunshine to give yourself that extra protection and keep the wrinkles away. Don't discard the sunblock, though!

Because of their sweetness, carrot juice is very useful to mix with other vegetable juices. And because of its lovely bright colour, children as well as adults find this easily digestible juice irresistable.

Buying and Storing

Choose firm carrots that are not too large – very large ones tend to be woody, taste earthy and contain little juice. Look for brightly coloured carrots as they will be the juiciest and sweetest. Never buy carrots that are soft, bendy or wrinkled, as they will be too old to have much nutritional value. Store carrots in a cool place and simply wash and dry organic carrots. Inorganic carrots should be well scrubbed and trimmed at both ends before juicing. This inexpensive vegetable is cheap and plentiful throughout the year.

FACT FILE

Generally speaking 500 g/1 lb of raw produce will give approximately 570 ml/1 pint of juice

---

CAULIFLOWER

The cauliflower is a member of the Brassica or cabbage family and the white part is the immature flowering head and stalk. This white part contains little beta-carotene compared to other members of this vegetable group and less riboflavin and folic acid. However, cauliflower does provide a good source of potassium and phosphorous, and is available all year round. Combining cauliflower with carrot juice makes it easier to digest.

47

Buying and Storing

The flower heads of the cauliflower should be tight, compact and a whitish colour – not yellowy or speckled with brown. The outer leaves should be bright green and springy and never limp. Wash, dry and store in the refrigerator. You have to use the cauliflower within a few days of purchase.

CELERY

Celery has notable healing qualities and was in fact first grown as a medicinal herb. It arrived in Britain in the seventeenth century in its cultivated form, but wild celery is indigenous to Britain and most of Europe.

Celery is an excellent source of organic sodium and as such is wonderful for fighting fatigue. Celery has a beneficial effect on the kidneys as it aids the elimination of waste via the urine. It has an anti-inflammatory quality which clears uric acid from painful joints, thereby helping rheumatism. Celery possesses similar properties to cabbage in that it treats stomach ulcers effectively and aids digestion. It is also well known for soothing the nerves, even helping to cure insomnia and headaches. For centuries celery has been depicted in folklore as having powers in the sexual field, acting as a stimulant.

Buying and Storing

Celery should be firm, erect and fresh looking, with leaves that look alive and not limp. I prefer the taste of the green ribs rather than the almost white varieties. Wash, dry and store in the refrigerator until needed. Celery is available all year round.

COURGETTES

Courgettes are similar to cucumbers in a nutritional sense. They are great thirst quenchers, cool and act like an internal body brush, cleansing the whole system. An excellent source of silicon, the courgette helps to keep us looking and feeling fit and young. It is a good juice for mixing, especially with carrot and garlic.

Buying and Storing

Choose the smaller courgettes as they will be juicier and less prone to bitterness. Wash, dry and refrigerate. Courgettes are available most of the year.

CUCUMBER

Cucumbers originally came from southern Asia and for over 3000 years have been grown in India. Ancient Egypt, Greece and Rome also valued the cucumber for its refreshing, cooling effect. This vegetable is 96 per cent water, making it wonderful for flushing out the system.

Cucumbers are an excellent source of the anti-ageing mineral silicon. This rejuvenate keeps our skin elastic, making it appear smoother and more youthful. Nails become stronger and healthier and the hair shinier and thicker as it promotes their growth.

Cucumbers contain relatively high levels of potassium, manganese, sulphur and chlorine, making them a valuable vegetable for juicing for both beauty and health. They are wonderful on their own or in combination with other juices.

Buying and Storing

Choose firm, dark green cucumbers free from soft ends, soft spots or wrinkles. The skin should be nobbly rather than smooth. Sometimes the cucumber is waxed and therefore it should be peeled prior to juicing or simply washed if it is organic. Dry and place in the refrigerator until required. They are available all year round.

FENNEL

I adore the aniseed flavour of fennel – it's so unusual and distinctly different. Most people just think of fennel as a herb, but the fleshy bulb makes a great vegetable for salads, accompaniments and of course, for juicing.

Fennel is similar to celery in a nutritional sense, and belongs to the same family. Fennel is a good source of beta-carotene, vitamin C and the B vitamins. Good levels of the minerals calcium and iron are also present. Like celery, it aids the digestive system and is especially beneficial when mixed with apple juice. It is also helpful in relieving headaches.

Buying and Storing

The feathery type leaves at the top of the fennel bulb should be present and look lively and bright green. The bulb should be white, firm and solid and free from wrinkling, dryness or brown marks, Fennel should be washed, dried and stored in the refrigerator. Fennel is available all year round.

GARLIC

Garlic has almost mystical powers and has been linked with sexual performance. It's the oldest aphrodisiac around – the ancient Greeks swore by it and who am I to disagree?

Garlic has a valued reputation as a natural healing plant for a variety of health problems. It is a known cancer, stroke and heart disease fighter, and is extremely valuable in lowering cholesterol and blood pressure levels. It also acts as an anticoagulant, keeping the blood thin and less prone to clotting. Garlic successfully treats rheumatism, arthritis, gout, respiratory diseases such as asthma, urinary problems, digestive disorders, colds, bronchitis and other lung infections and gives an important boost to our natural immune system. It's a pretty impressive little plant and adds a wonderful kick to juice.

Buying and Storing

The garlic bulb should consist of firm plump cloves and the tissue-like covering should be white and free from black or grey marks. Never buy soft garlic bulbs. Garlic should be stored at room temperature, preferably in a ventilated ceramic or terracotta container. Garlic is available all year round.

GINGER-ROOT

Ginger is far more popular in the east than here in the west and dates back to ancient times for the fame of its healing qualities as well as its pungent flavour. Its flavour makes it extremely useful for juicing, as it adds a nice bite to some of the more bland-tasting juices. Ginger is good for throat and vocal problems such as laryngitis and it is also effective as an expectorant of mucus and phlegm, and for preventing the onset of colds.

Ginger is an antiseptic spice which aids digestion and seems particularly useful for treating nausea, especially motion sickness, for which apple and ginger is a very useful combination of juices.

Buying and Storing

Ginger-root is a light brown knobbly root which should be dry and firm. Store in a cool dry place. Peel the root prior to juicing. Ginger-root is available all year round from supermarkets and grocers.

KALE

Kale is simply an abundance of dark curly leaves which is nutritionally very similar to cabbage. It is full of nutrients including a high level of calcium, selenium, potassium, silicon, vitamin C, beta-carotene, zinc, niacin, iron and some of the B vitamins.

Kale juice is good protection against cancer, heart disease, strokes and high blood pressure and helps to relieve arthritis pain. The high calcium content makes it useful in preventing osteoporosis and building healthy bones.

Buying and Storing

Leaves should look fresh, bright, deep green and crisp. It should be washed and dried before storing in the refrigerator. Kale is available from November to May.

FACT FILE

Form leafy vegetables into balls before pushing through the feed tube of the juicer

---

Lettuce

Lettuce dates back to ancient times with seeds having been found in plant remains in some ancient Egyptian tombs.

Rich in vitamin C, beta-carotene and the minerals silicon, sulphur and chlorine, the lettuce is a useful vegetable to juice. The silicon is especially beneficial for beauty, as it promotes hair growth and strength and keeps the complexion of the skin, clear and youthful. Add to this the B complex and folic acid present in lettuce and it really does contribute to a good skin. And of course, the folic acid helps to combat anaemia.

Buying and Storing

The darker the leaf, the more nutrients it contains. Look for crisp, fresh lettuce heads. It should be washed and dried before storing in the refrigerator. Lettuce is available all year round.

Onions

Onions date back at least 5000 years as a food and flavouring agent. They are related to garlic and have the same high reputation of being able to cure anything. Onions have been shown, again like garlic, to act as an anticoagulant and to reduce the harmful LDL, low density lipoprotein, cholesterol level in the blood, and to increase the good HDL, high density lipoprotein, level. Arthritis, rheumatism and gout are all treated effectively by onions as are anaemia, bronchitis, asthma and various urinary infections.

The old wives' tale about eating boiled onions in wintertime, and drinking their cooking liquor, holds some truth as onions are good for warding off the common cold and its symptoms. Onions are also thought to fight fatigue and aid digestion. Bear in mind one maxim: a little onion goes a long way. Add only a few peeled onion slices to the juices otherwise it will be unpalatable!

Buying and Storing

Choose onions which are firm and solid with dry papery skins. Keep in a cool dry place. They are available all year.

PARSLEY

Parsley has been grown in Britain since the sixteenth century and was extensively used by the ancient Greeks and Romans for its medicinal properties. It is extremely nutritious, containing most of the vitamins and minerals. Two grams of parsley can supply the daily recommended allowance of vitamin C. It is a good source of beta-carotene, potassium, sulphur, calcium, magnesium and iron. Life-giving chlorophyll is also present, which purifies the blood and cleanses the kidneys, liver and urinary tract.

Parsley has been used by herbalists for a long time as a diuretic and was in fact given to soldiers suffering from kidney problems after dysentry during the First World War. It is useful in treating gout and rheumatism as this herb helps eliminate uric acid. Parsley also aids digestion.

Buying and Storing

Parsley should be bright green in colour, never yellow. Don't buy parsley that looks limp and lifeless – it's old. Wash parsley and dry well before storing in the refrigerator. Parsley is available all year round and is quite easy to grow yourself on a windowsill. It's easiest to juice by rolling into a tight ball and wrapping in a vegetable leaf.

PEPPERS

Members of the capsicum family, these green, red, orange and yellow peppers are becoming increasingly popular and are now available all year round from supermarkets and market stalls. When ripe, the sweet pepper is coloured red, yellow or orange, but a lot of peppers are eaten green. Peppers do not ripen once they have been picked. All peppers are a good source of beta-carotene, vitamin C and the anti-ageing mineral silicon which is good for the skin, nails and hair. Peppers are in fact one of the best beauty enhancers around.

Peppers have a strong and distinctive flavour, whatever their odour and sweetness, so be careful not to overdo it. I never use more than one third of a pepper in any one juice as it will completely overpower the taste buds. A nice combination is pepper with carrots and ginger-root.

Buying and Storing

Look for smooth, firm peppers that are crisp and alive with colour. Wash and dry them before storing in the refrigerator. Available all year.

POTATOES

For most people living in the western world, potatoes are a staple food in the diet. We only have to look at how populations, such as the Irish, have survived on almost nothing else for many years in times of famine, to see the nutritional value of this underrated vegetable.

Eighty per cent of the weight of a potato is water and 20 per cent starch. It has a totally undeserved reputation as being a fattening food. The potato itself is a low-calorie food, containing just 100 calories per 100 grams – it is the fat and sauces we add to this humble vegetable that pile on the weight and inches. Potatoes provide vitamin C, B complex vitamins, calcium, iron and potassium. All the nutrients are found in or near to the skin of the potato.

The rich source of potassium in the potato makes it useful for treating high blood pressure. In fact, in many countries a tea made from potato peelings is given as a treatment to patients suffering from this condition. Potatoes are also though to be useful in treating stomach ulcers and arthritis. Potato juice needs mixing with other juices to make it palatable. Try adding carrots, lemon juice, garlic or parsley for extra flavour.

Buying and Storing

Buy firm potatoes which have no green tints on them. Scrub potatoes very well, dry and store in a cool dry place. There's no need to peel before juicing. Potatoes are available all year.

RADISHES

Radishes date back to at least Egyptian times when they were a very popular food. They contain significant amounts of potassium, magnesium, sodium, sulphur, a little vitamin C and some of the B complex vitamins. It has been found that the radish stimulates the discharge of bile which has a strong positive effect on the gall bladder. These small red orbs also clear sinus passages and have a soothing effect on sore throats.

Radish juice is very potent stuff and has a very distinct flavour. It is better mixed with other juices and used sparingly. Radishes are available most of the year.

Buying and Storing

Radishes should be bright, firm and crisp – never wrinkled and soft with wilting tops. As soon as you buy them, cut off their green tops. Wash and store in the refrigerator. Radishes will keep for about one week and are available all year round.

FACT FILE

Pulp from juicing can be used on the garden as compost

SPINACH

The nutritional qualities of spinach are legendary and for me are inextricably tied up with the cartoon character Popeye the Sailorman! Its reputation is well deserved for it contains not only significant amounts of iron but also potassium, calcium, sodium, magnesium, B complex vitamins, especially folic acid, vitamin C, and large quantities of beta-carotene. Spinach is a great cancer fighter, keeps the bowel active and is good for improving the circulation.

Spinach is extremely rich in chlorophyll, the life-giving substance in plants, which is beneficial to people suffering from anaemia and fatigue, or under mental strain. Spinach contains uric acid, so should be avoided by people suffering from rheumatism, arthritis and gout.

Buying and Storing

Spinach should be a dark green colour and look crisp, fresh and lively. Avoid spinach that is yellowing. Wash well, dry and store in the refrigerator. Spinach is available from March to December.

TOMATOES

I never know whether to call tomatoes a fruit or a vegetable. Strictly speaking they are a fruit but nobody seems to consider them as such. So here they are under vegetables!

Tomatoes were introduced to Europe in the sixteenth century from South America. They have appreciable amounts of vitamin C and beta-carotene, potassium, phosphorus and sulphur are also present to nourish our bodies. Tomato juice is especially nice mixed with either celery or cucumber. This delicious juice has a bright colour which makes it especially appealing to children.

Buying and Storing

Tomatoes should be a bright, vibrant red and feel heavy and firm but not hard. Wash, dry and refrigerate. Tomatoes are widely available all year.

WATERCRESS

Watercress is related to the nasturtium and both share the distinctive peppery taste given by the presence of benzyl mustard oil. This is a strong natural antibiotic of great benefit to maintaining the health of the gut. Watercress, like its other relatives broccoli and cabbage, is useful as protection against cancer and the presence of beta-carotene and Vitamin C enhances this role. This vegetable provides a useful source of folic acid, iodine and riboflavin.

Research has shown that watercress has helped people suffering from respiratory and urinary problems.

Buying and Storing

The watercress should be bright green and the leaves should look fresh and alive. Avoid yellowing, limp leaves. Wash, rinse, dry and store in the refrigerator. Watercress is available for much of the year.

CHAPTER FIVE

AND NOW FOR THE JUICES . . .

The recipes contained in the following chapters all have two things in common. Firstly, they are delicious and secondly, they are good for you in some way. As with any other type of recipe, the ingredients are not carved in stone but are adaptable. If you find you haven't enough pears for a particular juice then throw in an apple instead or should you be short on carrots, try parsnips. The idea is to improvise and experiment with your own combinations of produce. And all you have to do to ensure you are getting all the nutrients you want out of the juice is to check the vitamin and mineral content of the produce you intend to use.

The information is right here at your fingertips. You will probably find, as I did, that your favourite juices will contain your favourite fruits and vegetables. However, should you concoct a juice that you don't really care for, all you have to do is mix it with something else to change the taste. Why not try adding some mineral water, ice or skimmed milk powder? Simply use whatever you happen to have available at the time and see what the result is.

FACT FILE

Always process softer fruits and vegetables before firmer ones.
This will keep the strainer cleaner

I would suggest, however, that vegetable juices should not really be mixed with fruit juices as they tend not to give a good flavour. But, as with all general rules, there is the odd exception. Some vegetable juices can taste a little bitter and so the addition of a little pear, apple, pineapple or melon will help. You will soon find which combinations work and which don't. It's just a matter of trial and error until you find which juices really appeal to your taste-buds the most.

The important thing to remember is to drink the juice straight away, as storing it will lead to a loss of valuable vitamins and minerals which defeats the object of the exercise.

How much juice you consume each day is up to you. I start the day with an energy packed fruit juice with my breakfast, followed by a vegetable juice mid-morning to ward off any hunger pangs, and to avoid snacking off high-calorie junk foods. With my lunch I drink another vegetable juice and a refreshing fruit juice mid-afternoon to boost my energy level. My evening meal is accompanied by a soothing vegetable juice and I sometimes end the day with a vegetable juice to aid sleep. Six juices a day may seem a lot but just think how many cups of tea and coffee you consume in a day. Drinking juices is far better for you.

It would be better to start your juicing regime gradually, maybe drinking a fruit juice and a vegetable juice for a few days before building up to five or six glasses each day. By doing this you will be giving your system time to adjust to the new regime.

Do make sure that you wash the produce very well with a biodegradable cleanser to remove the harmful chemicals. Organic produce just needs a quick rinse with cold water and then you are on your way. The outer rind of pineapples and melons should be removed if they have not been organically grown, as should grape stems. To save time, I always wash fruit and vegetables as soon as I get them home. It's a lot easier than leaving it until you are ready to juice. Read the instructions with your juicer to check whether the seeds and rinds of certain fruit and vegetables are acceptable to the machine as this tends to vary.

Tools of The Trade

A juicer works fast which means that you have to have everything planned, prepared and to hand. The first thing to ensure is that you have all the necessary equipment and utensils in your kitchen. I have found that the following list is essential to my juicing.

THE JUICING MACHINE: There are a number of propietary makes of juice extractors and whichever you choose it should become the focal point of your kitchen. As it will be used frequently it should sit on a handy surface, ideally near the waste disposal unit of your sink if you're lucky enough to have one.

Cleaning your juicer just couldn't be easier. And you don't even have to clean it between juices. Once a day, or when the hopper is full, is ample. I tend to pop a plastic carrier bag at the side of the juicer and tip the pulp of the produce on to that – then you can simply throw the bag away. All the removable parts of the machine can be washed in warm water. There is no mess, no fuss and it is cleaned in minutes.

CHOPPING BOARD: You will need a chopping board that is large enough to take all the produce you are juicing. I use a large slab of marble because it's easy to keep clean and the surface isn't damaged by the cutting action. Formica and polyethelene plastic chopping boards are adequate as well. Steer clear of wooden ones though, as they tend to harbour germs more easily.

KNIVES: A few good-quality sharp knives with various blade lengths are essential. They should be sharpened every couple of weeks. It does pay to purchase decent knives in the first place as they will last for longer and give you far better service than the cheaper ones. I prefer a set of knives that are kept in a wooden block rather than individual ones which get lost in drawers. At least I always know where they are when I need them! Good knives are a good long-term investment. Cheap knives will make your wrist and hand ache and you are far more likely to cut yourself with a blunt knife.

WEIGHING SCALES: It's a good idea to have some kitchen weighing scales handy. The ones that fix on to the wall are good, especially in a small kitchen, because they don't take up valuable work surface space, and again you always know where to find them.

MEASURING JUG: A measuring jug is invaluable as it's important to know how much juice you obtain from various quantities of fruit and vegetables. You will also be able to measure the amount of green juice accurately – remember you should only have one-third of green juice in a mixture at any one time.

SALAD SPINNER: These salad spinners are absolutely essential for juicing. Once you have washed and rinsed leafy vegetables you just pop them into the spinner and in no time at all the leaves are dry and undamaged. It saves a lot of time, effort and soggy leaves.

STORAGE CONTAINERS: Tupperware type containers are very useful for storing washed fruit and vegetables, as are glass containers covered with either clingfilm or a plastic lid of some kind. Glass is useful as it doesn't hold any odours from the stored produce. Plastic and polythene bags are good to use if you tie them securely.

VEGETABLE BRUSH: Vegetables such as potatoes and carrots will probably require scrubbing with a vegetable brush to remove soil and dirt from their skins.

STRAINER: If you prefer clear juice then simply strain it through a plastic, fine-meshed strainer or even through coffee filters.

BLENDER: A blender is invaluable for utilizing certain produce, such as bananas and avocados that are unsuitable to use in a juicing machine. Simply blend the banana and mix with another juice to make a deliciously thick and creamy drink. A blender mashes the produce, making a purée type substance which includes all the fibre as well as the juice. The juicer extracts the juice from the fibre, giving a liquid packed with nutrients that is absorbed by the body very quickly. The blended version will take your body hours to digest. Fibre is crucial to everyone, but you can easily obtain it from other sources.

NOTE ON QUANTITIES: All quantities given in the recipes section yield approximately one glass of juice. Note, however, that final quantities can vary depending on the size of the fruit and vegetables used.

CHAPTER SIX

BEAUTIFUL . . . NATURALLY

You are what you eat! I have always believed this, whether you are talking about health or beauty. Let's face it, our skin, hair, nails and eyes are the most visible parts of the body and as such shape our own self-image, not to mention how others see us.

Millions of pounds are eagerly spent each year on lotions and potions to enhance our beauty from the outside. Creams to make wrinkles disappear and smooth our skins. Conditioners to strengthen our hair and sprays to make it shine. Concoctions for bathing eyes for that sparkle and brightness. Nail preparations to harden and lengthen weak, brittle nails and transform them, hopefully, into talons.

We willingly invest all this money, time and effort in an attempt to be more attractive. And there is nothing at all wrong with that. We feel better, socialize more comfortably and act more confidently when we look our very best. So why not do the job much more effectively and save yourself pounds in the bargain? Juices are the active ingredients for natural beauty because they work from the inside out. By providing essential nutrients to our body, juices make our skin clearer, fresher and younger looking; our hair stronger and full of life; our eyes become brighter and more alive; and our nails longer and stronger. It just couldn't be easier and the results are rapid. Within a matter of weeks, you will look younger and healthier – and that is a promise!

When we feel under the weather or stressed out it is our visible parts that show the strain. The characteristic signs of dull, lifeless hair; heavy tired-looking eyes; weak, broken nails and a sallow complexion rear their ugly heads and give us away.

Our beauty also suffers increasingly from the environment in which we live. Pollution, central heating, the elements generally and self-abuse such as heavy smoking and drinking all take their toll. On top of this we bombard our bodies with convenience and junk foods full of fats, sugars and chemicals, containing little in the way of nutrients. These are the arch enemies of the body beautiful.

This chapter is packed full of delicious fruit and vegetable juices that will enhance your natural beauty. Juices for the skin, hair, nails and eyes – the all important, visible parts of our bodies.

So don't delay, start juicing today – it's the very best thing you could do for your looks!

The Beauty Boosters

SKIN DEEP

There is no doubt about it, a smooth unblemished skin glowing with good health is the envy of every woman, irrespective of age. A healthy skin is the basic ingredient for beauty and yet the majority find it quite elusive.

FACT FILE

One square inch of skin has a total of about 19,000,000 cells

---

Our skin isn't just a 'bodysuit', it acts like a mirror to reflect our general well being. The tell-tale signs of spots and pimples, dullness and grey pallor soon make their appearance when we feel under par. The same scenario occurs if we don't consume the necessary vitamins and minerals. It doesn't matter how much make-up we apply either, or how skilfully, the camouflage simply doesn't work. We can easily increase our beauty boosters by drinking fruit and vegetable juices high in certain nutrients. A fresh, glowing complexion with a smooth, youthful appearance can be yours! Boosting your vitamins A, B$_2$, C, and E and your potassium intake will help you to achieve this.

The embarrassing condition of acne is helped by drinking juices high in the mineral zinc. And if you want to emulate Peter Pan and be wrinkle-free, then enjoy the anti-ageing juices which contain a mixture of silicon, selenium, potassium and beta-carotene.

The rest is up to you – drink yourself to a beautiful skin!

FACT FILE

Our skin accounts for about 15 per cent of our body weight

The Recipes

ANTI-AGEING RECIPES

Youthdew

6 apricots
125 g/4 oz red grapes
1 passion fruit
1 mango

1. Cut the apricots in half and remove the stones.
2. Remove the stems from the grapes if they are not organic.
3. Cut the passion fruit in half and scoop out the inside.
4. Peel the mango and remove the stone.
5. Process the fruit in the juicer.

Cherry Wonder

125 g/4 oz cherries
1 apple
8 strawberries
sparkling mineral water

1. Cut the cherries in half and remove the stones.
2. Cut the apple into wedges.
3. Process all the fruit in the juicer.
4. Add mineral water to taste to give it a sparkle.

Wrinkle-Free

4 carrots
1 pear
6 lettuce leaves
1 handful of parsley

1. Trim the carrots.
2. Cut the pear into wedges.
3. Roll the lettuce leaves into balls.
4. Process all the ingredients in the juicer.

Smoothie

2 carrots
2 asparagus sticks
½ cucumber
½ raw beetroot

1. Trim the carrots and the asparagus stalks.
2. Cut the vegetables into workable lengths if necessary.
3. Process the ingredients in the juicer.

FACT FILE

Our skin measures approximately 22 square feet

ANTI-ACNE RECIPES

Spot-Free Zone

4 carrots
¼ green pepper
2 spring cabbage leaves
2.5 cm/1 in knob ginger-
    root, unpeeled
½ handful of parsley

1. Trim the carrots.
2. Cut the pepper into strips.
3. Roll the spring cabbage leaves into balls.
4. Process all the ingredients in the juicer.

Clear Skin Juice

4 carrots
25 g/1 oz spinach
25 g/1 oz kale

1. Trim the carrots.
2. Roll the spinach and kale leaves into balls.
3. Process the vegetables in the juicer.

The Cleanser

4 carrots
2 parsnips
1 cm/½ in knob ginger-root

1. Trim the carrots and parsnips.
2. Process all the vegetables in the juicer.

Flower Power

2 apples
3 cauliflower florets with
   stems
4 Brussels sprouts

1. Cut the apple into wedges.
2. Process all the ingredients in the juicer.

COMPLEXION AND HEALTHY SKIN RECIPES

Smooth as Silk

125 g/4 oz Cantaloup melon
2 peaches
2 Kiwi fruits, unpeeled

1. Cut the outer rind from the melon if it is not organic; cut the melon into strips.
2. Cut the peaches in half and remove the stones.
3. Process all the fruit in the juicer.

Skin Zinger

2 oranges
1 grapefruit
½ lime

1. Peel the fruit, leaving as much of the white pith on as possible. Cut into large chunks.
2. Process the fruit in the juicer.

Skin Glow

1 pineapple round, 2.5 cm/
   1 in thick
125 g/4 oz green grapes,
   with or without seeds
2 apples

1. Remove the skin from the pineapple if it is not organic. Cut the flesh into thin stripes.
2. Remove the stems from the grapes if they are not organic.
3. Cut the apples into wedges.
4. Process the fruit in the juicer.

Radiance

2 apples
2 celery sticks
4 watercress springs
1 small courgette

1. Cut the apples into wedges.
2. Cut the celery into workable lengths and trim the courgettes.
3. Process all the ingredients in the juicer.

Red Dazzler

225 g/8 oz watermelon
10 strawberries

1. Trim the outer skin from the watermelon if it isn't organic and cut the flesh into strips.
2. Process all the fruit in the juicer.

Satin Smooth

4 carrots
2 broccoli florets with stems
1 clove of garlic, peeled

1. Trim the carrots.
2. Process all the vegetables in the juicer.

Blooming Beauty

125 g/4 oz red grapes
10 strawberries

1. Remove the stems from the grapes if they are not organic.
2. Process all the fruit in the juicer.

Hair – Our Crowning Glory

Hair really is our crowning glory, and when we are in good health it is shinier, stronger and full of life. But when we don't receive the necessary nutrients, or we are ill, it tells in the condition of our hair. It becomes limp, lifeless and dull. Hair is a good indicator of our general well being. Each hair shaft gains nutrients and therefore life from the papilla located in the scalp – the power house of the hair. A good healthy head of shining hair can be achieved by drinking juices rich in the minerals phosphorus, sulphur and silicon. If you want to retard hair loss and premature greying try boosting your B complex vitamins. Good nutrition is a must for healthy looking hair.

FACT FILE

Hair grows approximately 2.5 cm/1 in every 2½ months

SHINING HAIR RECIPES

Glossy

¼ red pepper
6 lettuce leaves
4 carrots
1 handful of parsley

1. Cut the red pepper into strips.
2. Form the lettuce leaves into balls.
3. Trim the carrots.
4. Process all the vegetables in the juicer.

Wet Look

225 g/8 oz cherries
2 pears

1. Cut the cherries in half and remove the stones.
2. Cut the pears into wedges.
3. Process the fruit in the juicer.

FACT FILE

Hair grows faster in the heat of summer

HAIR STRENGTHENER AND HAIR GROWTH RECIPES

Hair Strengthener

4 carrots
3 cauliflower florets with stems

1. Trim the carrots.
2. Process both vegetables in the juicer.

Crowning Glory

8 apricots
½ cucumber

1. Halve the aprocots and remove the stones.
2. Process both ingredients in the juicer.

FACT FILE

You lose between 20 and 100 hairs each day under natural conditions

---

Rapido

¼ green pepper
3 apples
¼ cucumber
2 celery sticks
1 handful of parsley

1. Cut the pepper into strips.
2. Cut the apples into wedges.
3. Process all the ingredients in the juicer.

Staying Power

4 kale leaves
5 carrots
½ handful of parsley

1. Roll the kale leaves into balls.
2. Trim the carrots.
3. Process all the vegetables in the juicer.

FACT FILE

The only way to cure split ends is to cut them off!

Nails Know-How

Nicely shaped, manicured nails look attractive and classy. Broken, split, flaking nails can ruin an otherwise immaculate appearance. Yes, you can cover up your natural nails with falsies but why should you bother. Strengthen your own nails and turn them into an asset.

The hard visible part of the nail is essentially a structure of complex protein and gains its nutrients from the nail matrix located under the white half moon at the base of the nail. Our nails can tell us quite a lot about what is happening to our bodies. For example, soft transparent nails are associated with arthritis and white flecks with zinc deficiency. By consuming more of the nutrients that feed the nail, such as calcium, silicon, phosphorus and sulphur, you are building healthy looking strong nails.

FACT FILE

Fingernails grow about 1 cm/½ in each week – twice as fast as toenails

---

Talons

4 carrots
2 kale leaves
¼ cucumber
3 watercress sprigs

1. Trim the carrots.
2. Form the kale leaves into balls.
3. Process all the vegetables in the juicer.

Nail Strengthener

4 lettuce leaves
¼ green pepper
4 carrots
1 parsnip

1. Form the lettuce leaves into balls.
2. Cut the green pepper into strips.
3. Trim the carrots and parsnip.
4. Process all the vegetables in the juicer.

FACT FILE

It takes approximately three months for fingernails to grow out completely

Nail Guard

4 carrots
½ cucumber
1 handful of parsley

1. Trim the carrots.
2. Process all the vegetables in the juicer.

Shiny and Strong

6 apricots
125 g/4 oz cherries
1 pear

1. Halve the apricots and cherries and remove the stones.
2. Cut the pear into wedges.
2. Process the fruit in the juicer.

Strong and Long

2 spinach leaves
3 apples
2 broccoli florets with stems
1 cm/½ in knob ginger-root

1. Form the spinach leaves into balls.
2. Cut the apples into wedges.
3. Process all the ingredients in the juicer.

FACT FILE

Nail growth slows down as we get older

Bright Eyes

The eyes are the window to one's soul, and I must admit that the eyes have it for me every time. Eyes are *the* feature I always notice about people. Bright, sparkling, appealing eyes are probably the sexiest facial feature to the opposite sex. And there is no amount of make-up that will conceal eye strain or tiredness, so it is well worth looking after such an important attribute.

Our eyes take a regular hammering when you think of it. Exposure to the elements – cold winds and sunshine – close eye work such as reading, watching television for hours, driving a vehicle, all take their toll on our eyes. And when we feel tired or under the weather it shows in our eyes, making them a little red, puffy, heavy looking and dull. Our vision may also become impaired as we find it increasingly difficult to see in the dark or we may experience blurred vision.

To make our eyes both more beautiful and healthy we need to consume juices rich in vitamin A, commonly called beta-carotene. The benefits will be clearly evident within a few weeks of drinking such juices regularly.

FACT FILE

Winston Churchill, during the Second World War, issued a propoganda statement that our servicemen could see in the dark due to a diet rich in carrots. This was an attempt to conceal our secret weapon – RADAR. There was more truth in that carrot statement than was realized

---

Eye Recipes

RECIPES FOR NIGHTBLINDNESS

Eyes That See In The Dark

5 carrots
50 g/2 oz fennel

1. Trim the carrots.
2. Cut the fennel into wedges.
3. Process both vegetables in the juicer.

Radar Vision

350 g/12 oz Cantaloup melon

1. Cut the outer rind from the melon if it is not organic.
2. Cut the flesh into strips.
3. Process in the juicer.

CLEAR EYE RECIPES

Brighteyes

1 mango
175 g/6 oz strawberries
175 g/6 oz raspberries
sparkling mineral water

1. Peel and remove the stone from the mango.
2. Process all the fruits in the juicer.
3. Add mineral water to taste to give the juice a nice bubble.

RECIPES FOR TIRED AND IRRITATED EYES

The Sparkler

6 carrots
4 sprigs of watercress

1. Trim the carrots.
2. Process the ingredients in the juicer.

Eye Beautifier

4 carrots
2 kale leaves
½ handful of parsley

1. Trim the carrots.
2. Form the kale leaves into balls.
3. Process all the ingredients in the juicer.

FOR GENERAL EYESIGHT

Twenty-Twenty Vision

6 apricots
1 peach
175 g/6 oz Cantaloup melon

1. Halve the apricots and the peach and remove the stones.
2. Remove the outer skin from the melon if it is not organic.
3. Cut the flesh of the melon into strips.
4. Process the fruit in the juicer.

Sight Enhancer

4 carrots
2 apples
½ handful of parsley

1. Trim the carrots.
2. Cut the apples into wedges.
3. Process all the ingredients in the juicer.

CHAPTER SEVEN

SEXY JUICES

C an sexual desire and performance be enhanced by consuming certain foods and nutrients? Throughout history the answer to this question has been an emphatic 'Yes!' The ancient Greeks worshipped a goddess of love for whom they made various concoctions and potions. She was called Aphrodite, and her name was given to aphrodisiacs. These can be literally anything from foods and potions to charms and lotions associated with increasing one's sexual desire, enhancing sexual performance or arousing excitement and lust.

FACT FILE

Onions were banned from the ancient Egyptian diet because they were thought to drive people mad with passion!

Eastern civilizations have, for centuries, advocated certain foods for provoking erotic desires. After all those years, who are we to say there is no connection between the foods we eat and our love lives? I for one definitely believe in the potential power of aphrodisiacs. After all, what have we got to lose?

We are familiar with the more famous aphrodisiacs such as oysters, but what about celery, asparagus and fennel? Well, there are many fruits and vegetables that have sexually enhancing properties associated with them. And the beauty of them is you can purchase them from supermarkets, and nobody will know what you are planning!

Scepticism is rife amongst the medical profession regarding aphrodisiacs, and yet a great many of the substances contain elements known to be sex enhancers. Celery, for example, has been known as an aphrodisiac in France since the eighteenth century and in recent times has been found to contain pheromones which act to stimulate sexual desire. In fact, you can even buy perfumes today with pheromones as the base scent to arouse the passions. And the vegetable fennel is an active ingredient in many modern day aphrodisiac preparations and dates back to Roman times. As with most old wives' tales, there does seem to be some truth in the claims made. After all, there is never smoke without fire . . .

Many sexual problems have been linked with a deficiency in the mineral zinc. In particular, impotency has been associated with a lack of this mineral, along with lack of the vitamins A and E. Vitamin E is being increasingly recommended to boost your sex drive, ensuring healthy sexual functioning and increasing your stamina. In fact, the claims made for vitamin E are so far-reaching that it has become known as the miracle vitamin.

The best thing you can do to give your sex life a zing is to consume juices rich in the vitamins A and E and the mineral zinc. Avoid tea and coffee because caffeine may inhibit absorption of minerals and vitamins. Let's face it, increasing our intake of these nutrients can only enhance our basic diet which is the basis for any vigorous and fulfilling sex life.

The Recipes

RECIPES TO ENHANCE YOUR SEXUAL DESIRE

The Sex Booster

3 apples
2.5 cm/1 in knob of ginger-
  root
2 celery sticks

1. Cut the apples into wedges.
2. Peel and slice the ginger-root.
3. Process all the ingredients in the juicer.

The Bunnyhop

4 spinach leaves
4 carrots
½ handful of parsley

1. Roll the spinach leaves into balls.
2. Trim the carrots.
3. Process all the ingredients in the juicer.

Love Nectar

2 pineapple rounds, 2.5 cm/
   1 in thick
5 apricots
1 mango

1. Remove the outer rind from the pineapple if it is inorganic and cut the flesh into strips.
2. Halve the apricots and remove the stones.
3. Peel the mango and remove the stone.
4. Process all the fruit in the juicer.

Feeling Fruity

175 g/6 oz cherries
175 g/6 oz strawberries

1. Halve the cherries and remove the stones.
2. Process all the fruit in the juicer.

Screwdriver

1 orange
50 g/2 oz rosehips
125 g/4 oz blackcurrants

1. Remove the rind from the orange, leaving as much of the white pith as you can.
2. Break the orange into large segments.
3. Process all the fruit in the juicer.

Citrus Awakener

2 oranges
½ grapefruit
½ lime

1. Remove the rind from the citrus fruits, leaving as much of the white pith as possible.
2. Break the fruits into large segments.
3. Process the fruit in the juicer.

Love Juice

5 carrots
4 kale leaves
2 onion slices, peeled

1. Trim the carrots.
2. Form the kale leaves into balls.
3. Process all the vegetables in the juicer.

Aphrodite

2 apples
4 asparagus sticks
3 celery sticks
2 onion slices, peeled

1. Cut the apples into wedges.
2. Cut celery into workable lengths.
3. Process all the ingredients in the juicer.

Love In A Mist

1 fennel bulb
4 carrots
2 cloves of garlic, peeled
½ handful of parsley

1. Cut the fennel into wedges.
2. Trim the carrots.
3. Process all the vegetables in the juicer.

Love Potion

175 g/6 oz red grapes
3 peaches

1. Remove the stems from the grapes if they are not organic.
2. Halve the peaches and remove the stones.
3. Process both fruits in the juicer.

FACT FILE

Grapes are strongly associated with sex as they have been eaten at orgies throughout history. Just look at the Romans!

STAMINA BOOSTING RECIPES

All Systems Go

2 pineapple rounds, 2.5 cm/
  1 in thick
2 celery sticks
3 radishes

1. Remove the outer skin from the pineapple if inorganic and cut the flesh into strips.
2. Process all the ingredients in the juicer.

The Booster

4 carrots
2 apples
½ handful of parsley

1. Trim the carrots.
2. Cut the apples into wedges.
3. Process all the ingredients in the juicer.

Staying Power

4 carrots
4 Brussels sprouts
2 celery sticks

1. Trim the carrots.
2. Process all the ingredients in the juicer.

CHAPTER EIGHT

CANCER

Cancer is probably the most feared of all diseases prevalent in our society today. The 'Big C' not only kills, it causes extensive suffering to the victim, and to friends and relatives. And the treatments for cancer can be severely brutal both in a physical and an emotional sense. Most people will know someone who has either died from this killer disease or who has suffered an amputation of a limb or breast, and who has had to undergo the very unpleasant, debilitating treatment of chemotherapy, with the resulting loss of all body hair.

Cancer is a malignant tumour that occurs when cells divide in an abnormal and unconventional manner, which then invade the healthy surrounding tissue, destroying it. The use of vitamins and minerals in addition to conventional therapy can be of great benefit to sufferers. Research has found that certain foods and types of diet patterns are important in causing various forms of cancer. Populations who gain most of their protein from animal sources tend to have a high incidence of cancer, especially of the bowel.

Diets rich in meat also tend to be low in fibre and high in saturated fat, which is strongly linked to breast cancer. Meat also contains chemicals in the forms of hormones, antibiotics and tenderizers, which may be carcinogenic. Processed meats, such as sausages, luncheon meat and salami are treated with nitrites and nitrates, and have high levels of saturated fat and salt, which are carcinogenic. Smoked, salted, cured, pickled and barbecued foods such as bacon, kippers and foods in brine are all cancer promoters – especially of the stomach.

Refined carbohydrates such as white flour, white rice, sugar, white spaghetti and pasta are all low in fibre and contain little in the form of nutrients. These products are nothing more than empty calories.

The additives that are crammed into much of our foods these days are increasingly being linked with cancer. Artificial sweeteners and all coal-tar dyes are the ones to particularly avoid. And of course, consuming alcohol and caffeine inhibits our ability to absorb nutrients, thereby depleting our body reserves.

The evidence is overwhelming and the path perfectly clear. In order to reduce the incidence of cancer we need to reduce our intake of saturated fat, salt, smoked, cured and pickled foods, reduce our caffeine and alcohol intake, and increase our fibre. At the same time, our consumption of fresh fruit and vegetables and wholegrains needs to be increased. The juices in this section are particularly useful in guarding against cancer and in their treatment because they are rich in beta-carotene, vitamins C and E and the mineral selenium. All these nutrients are important and effective antioxidants that scavenge the body seeking out and destroying free radical molecules. These molecules are dangerous because they are prone to developing malignancies and are thought to be carcinogenic.

Beta-carotene is considered to be important in the fight against cancer because its antioxidant qualities help combat degenerative or free radical activity in the body. It is also thought to suppress the formation of malignant cells damaged by carcinogens. The vitamin has been found especially useful in protecting against cancer of the lungs, larynx, oesophagus and bladder.

Vitamins C and E are also antioxidants and protectors, but act in a different way to beta-carotene. These vitamins act like a wall in the body to block the formation of carcinogens from substances such as nitrosomes formed from nitrates in food. Cancer of the bladder, breast, stomach, oesophagus and colon have been found to be those most protected by these vitamins.

It is crucial that the diet of anyone, either suffering from cancer or in a high-risk category, contains all the necessary vitamins and minerals. There is one trace mineral in particular however that stands out in the prevention and treatment of cancer. That mineral is selenium. Plants absorb selenium from the soil and it is the level of selenium in the soil that determines how much of the mineral is present in local diets. It varies widely from area to area.

Epidemiological evidence suggests that populations living in low selenium areas have a higher incidence of cancer than comparable populations in high selenium areas. In animal experiments it has been found that some cancers can be successfully treated by the antioxidant trace element selenium. The mineral appears to toughen the cell membrane, thereby making it more resilient against attackers. Selenium also stimulates the immune system, which protects against cancer. Selenium could be defined as the self-defence system in cells of the body.

The Recipes

Surprise Juice

6 apricots
6 lychees
2 apples

1. Halve the apricots and remove the stones.
2. Peel the lychees and remove the stones.
3. Cut the apples into wedges.
4. Process all the fruit in the juicer.

Berry Booster

175 g/6 oz raspberries
175 g/6 oz blackberries
sparkling mineral water

1. Process all the fruit in the juicer.
2. Add mineral water to taste to add a nice bubble.

Melon Juice

175 g/6 oz Cantaloup melon
175 g/6 oz watermelon

1. Remove the outer skins from the melons if they are inorganic.
2. Cut the flesh into strips.
3. Process the melons in the juicer.

Wonder Juice

5 carrots
1 beetroot
4 watercress sprigs
1 clove of garlic, peeled

1. Trim the carrots.
2. Cut the beetroot into wedges if necessary.
3. Process all the vegetables in the juicer.

Cabbage Patch Juice

4 spinach leaves
4 carrots
7.5 cm/3 in wedge of green cabbage
¼ potato, scrubbed

1. Form the spinach leaves into balls.
2. Trim the carrots.
3. Process all the vegetables in the juicer.

Broccoli Booster

5 carrots
4 kale leaves
2 broccoli florets

1. Trim the carrots.
2. Form the kale leaves into balls.
3. Process all the vegetables in the juicer.

Tomato Tansy

3 tomatoes
7.5 cm/3 in wedge of green cabbage
1 clove of garlic, peeled

1. Process all the ingredients in the juicer.

Whiter Shade of Pale

2 pineapple rounds, 2.5 cm/
   1 in thick
2 apples
1 mango

1. Remove the outer skin from the pineapple if it is not organic and cut the flesh into strips.
2. Cut the apples into wedges.
3. Peel the mango and remove the stone.
4. Process the fruit in the juicer.

Citrus Dream

2 oranges
1 tangerine
¼ lemon
1 peach
sparkling mineral water

1. Peel the citrus fruits, leaving as much white pith as possible on the fruit. Break into large segments.
2. Cut the peach in half and remove the stone.
3. Process the fruit in the juicer.
4. Add mineral water to taste to give it a good sparkle.

Limey

1 grapefruit
¼ lime
2 apples

1. Peel the citrus fruits, leaving as much of the white pith on the fruit as possible. Break into large segments.
2. Cut the apples in wedges.
3. Process the fruit in the juicer.

Red Delight

1 apple
75 g/3 oz red grapes
125 g/4 oz cranberries
sparkling mineral water

1. Cut the apple into wedges
2. Remove the stems from the grapes if they are not organic.
3. Process all the fruit in the juicer.
4. Add mineral water to taste.

CHAPTER NINE

HEART DISEASE

Heart disease remains the number one cause of premature death in the western world even though health education programmes have been instituted on a worldwide scale. Approximately one Briton dies each and every three minutes of the day and night from heart disease and it kills 3 in 10 of all men and 2 in 10 of all women. That amounts to a staggering 175,793 people each year – it's like a jumbo jet containing 480 people crashing each day and killing every one of them. A frightening thought, isn't it? The story doesn't end there. About 300,000 people suffer a heart attack each year and 320,000 consult their doctor with angina. The heart disease problem is immense, and no one is immune from attack.

There remains no doubt whatsoever that diet is the major cause – diets that are too high in fat, especially the saturated type, sugar and salt, and too low in fibre. The evidence is clear that improved nutrition is the vital key to both the effective treatment and prevention of chronic heart disease. The good news is that we can do something positive to combat this mass killer.

International research confirms that countries with high animal fat intake also have high death rates from chronic heart disease, whilst countries where fruit and vegetables dominate the diet, the mortality rate from chronic heart disease is much lower.

In countries such as America, Finland and Australia, this information was acted upon and health education programmes were actively pursued. The result was that deaths from chronic heart disease fell dramatically in these countries. Unfortunately, in other countries, like Britain, the attempt has been positively feeble with little or no commitment to such health education programmes. It comes as no surprise therefore that we are top of the world league for heart disease deaths. The contrasts could not be more vivid. Men aged 35 to 74 in England and Wales have a 200 per cent higher chance of dying from chronic heart disease than their Italian counterparts; 300 per cent higher that their French contemporaries; and a staggering 800 per cent more than their opposite numbers in Japan. These are not figures to be proud of.

The Prevention Plan

Looking at the heart in a very simplistic way, it is nothing more than a very efficient pump, beating some 100,000 times every twenty-four hours. The major cause of chronic heart disease, an unhealthy diet, leads to the arteries to and from the heart becoming blocked by cholesterol and fatty deposits. Quite literally, they become narrowed and hardened, obstructing the flow of blood carrying oxygen and nutrients to the heart muscle. Sometimes the blood cannot find an alternative route, which results in part of the heart muscle dying – a heart attack. It is fatal if a large area of the heart is affected.

We can minimize the risks of heart disease as well as treat it by reducing saturated fats, sugar and salt in our diets, and increasing the intake of fibre. But we can do much more than this because certain vitamins and minerals have been found extremely useful in both the prevention and treatment of the disease. The protective vitamins are C and E along with the minerals calcium, potassium, selenium and magnesium.

Interestingly, people living in hard-water areas appear to suffer less from heart disease than those living in soft-water areas, and the main minerals in hard water are calcium and magnesium. Thus, they are thought to have a protective effect. Post-mortem studies performed on people who have died from heart disease indicate lower heart muscle levels of magnesium than present in those who have died of other causes.

Potassium levels in the heart muscle have also been found to be low in those who have died suddenly from heart attacks; and low potassium levels are also associated with angina.

The main mineral in recent years to have captured people's attention is selenium. In the animal world a deficiency in this mineral leads to heart problems and high blood pressure. In human studies it has been found that those living in areas where soil selenium levels are low, and therefore selenium intakes low, chronic heart disease is high. A trial undertaken in China involved over 45,000 people who lived in a low selenium area and where chronic heart disease was very high. Supplementing the diet of thousands of children reduced the rate of those already suffering from chronic heart disease from 50 per cent to 6 per cent. Of all the minerals, selenium really does appear to be the miracle worker.

Vitamin E is an efficient antioxidant, as is vitamin C, fighting free radical activity in the body and thereby guarding against cardiovascular disorders. Free radical activity occurs when harmful chemicals, free radicals, are produced when oily or fatty foods react with oxygen turning them rancid. Free radicals are irritants and thought to be carcinogenic. Vitamin E also protects polyunsaturated fatty acids in the blood which are thought to reduce the chances of heart disease and decrease the possibility of further problems for those who have the complaint. Vitamin E also helps the important mineral selenium to function effectively.

The Recipes

Orange Swirl

3 large oranges

1. Remove the rind from the oranges leaving as much of the white pith as possible.
2. Process in the juicer.

The Stair Climber

2 apples
3 pears

1. Cut the apples and pears into wedges.
2. Process the fruit in the juicer.

Sparkler

3 peaches
125 g/4 oz cherries
sparkling mineral water

1. Cut the peaches and cherries in half and remove the stones.
2. Process the fruit in the juicer.
3. Add mineral water to taste.

Bananarama

1 banana
2 pineapple rounds, 2.5 cm/
   1 in thick
1 pear

1. Blend the banana in a food processor or blender.
2. Remove the outer skin from the pineapple if it is not organic. Cut the flesh into strips.
3. Cut the pear into wedges.
4. Process the pineapple and pear in the juicer and mix the juice with the banana in the blender, giving it a quick whirl.

Wonder Juice

4 carrots
7.5 cm/3 in wedge of green
   cabbage
¼ small onion, peeled

1. Trim the carrots.
2. Process all the vegetables in the juicer.

Kick Back Juice

4 apples
4 broccoli florets and stems

1. Cut the apples into wedges.
2. Process both ingredients in the juicer.

The Defender

4 kale leaves
4 carrots
1 clove of garlic, peeled

1. Form the kale leaves into balls.
2. Trim the carrots.
3. Process all the ingredients in the juicer.

The Equalizer

3 apples
4 sprigs watercress
2 tomatoes
1 handful parsley

1. Cut the apples into wedges.
2. Process all the ingredients in the juicer.

The Fighter

2 apples
1 pear
2 celery sticks

1. Cut the apples and pear into wedges.
2. Process all the ingredients in the juicer.

The Bodyguard

5 carrots
2 pears
2.5 cm/1 in knob ginger-
   root

1. Trim the carrots.
2. Cut the pears into wedges.
3. Process all the ingredients in the juicer.

CHAPTER TEN

CHOLESTEROL

Once upon a time the medical profession was deeply divided about the casual link between cholesterol and blocked arteries. Today, however, the controversy has virtually disappeared. Overwhelming evidence concludes that cholesterol, which is a fatty substance, clings to the artery walls, thereby narrowing them. Cholesterol acts in two ways. Firstly, by narrowing the artery walls it makes it increasingly difficult for the blood to flow freely. Secondly, it makes the blood thicker and more prone to clotting. The body needs cholesterol in small amounts and manufactures it itself. Raised blood cholesterol levels are affected mainly by dietary factors, but alcohol, stress and smoking are also thought to play a part.

One type of cholesterol, HDL, high density lipoprotein, is actually good for us, whilst the other type, LDL, low density lipoprotein, is bad news. Certain nutrients have been found particularly useful in reducing raised blood cholesterol levels. Vitamin E has been shown to protect polyunsaturated fatty acids in the blood from being destroyed, so increasing the beneficial HDL type of cholesterol. Vitamin C also reduces raised blood cholesterol levels; and garlic is renowned for its ability to achieve this too. Adequate intakes of calcium seem to lower both fat and cholesterol levels in the blood. This mineral appears to operate by reducing the LDL cholesterol levels, whilst allowing the HDL cholesterol levels to be maintained. Niacin, part of the B vitamin group, has also been shown to be quite effective in lowering cholesterol. It appears to suppress the synthesis of cholesterol in the body.

Drinking juices rich in these nutrients will be beneficial in the fight against Public Enemy Number One.

The Recipes

Cholesterol Blow-Out

6 carrots
1 handful parsley
2 cloves of garlic, peeled

1. Trim the carrots.
2. Process all the ingredients in the juicer.

Cholesterol Buster

4 kale leaves
4 apples
4 sprigs of watercress

1. Form the kale leaves into balls.
2. Cut the apples into wedges.
3. Process all the ingredients in the juicer.

Cholesterol Cure Juice

4 carrots
2 celery sticks
¼ small onion, peeled
2.5 cm/1 in knob ginger-
   root

1. Trim the carrots.
2. Process all the ingredients in the juicer.

The Reducer

1 pineapple round, 2.5 cm/
   1 in thick
2 apples
2 Kiwi fruit
sparkling mineral water

1. Remove the outer skin from the pineapple if it is not organic, and cut the flesh into strips.
2. Cut the apples into wedges.
3. Process all the fruit in the juicer.
4. Add sparkling mineral water to taste to give the juice a bubble.

Red Alert

175 g/6 oz watermelon
2 passion fruit
125 g/4 oz strawberries

1. Remove the outer rind from the watermelon if it is not organic and cut the flesh into strips.
2. Cut the passion fruit in half and scoop out the inside.
3. Process all the fruit in the juicer.

The Cholesterol Clear-Out

1 ruby red grapefruit
2 tangerines
2 pineapple rounds, 2.5 cm/
   1 in thick

1. Remove the skin from the grapefruit and tangerines, leaving as much of the white pith as you can.
2. Break the citrus fruit into large segments.
3. Remove the outer skin from the pineapple if it is not organic and cut the flesh into strips.
4. Process the fruit in the juicer.

Pectin Punch

4 apples
1 pear
1 orange

1. Cut the apples and pear into wedges.
2. Remove the peel from the orange and break the fruit into large segments.
3. Process the fruit in the juicer.

CHAPTER ELEVEN

STROKES

A stroke occurs when the brain is damaged by an obstruction such as a blood clot in an artery, due to atherosclerosis of brain blood vessels or to high blood pressure creating a ruptured artery. The result is usually paralysis on one side of the body and speech is often affected. Strokes remain an important cause of death in Britain, accounting for 9 per cent of all male and 15 per cent of all female deaths. 100,000 people have a stroke every year and over one-third are permanently disabled by it.

Once again, a switch from saturated to polyunsaturated fatty acids is a good move. The vitamins C and E have been shown to be useful as a preventative measure and in the treatment of the condition. These vitamins help to develop strong and healthy blood vessels and capillaries, and therefore protect the body against strokes. Vitamin E also helps to keep the blood thin and less sticky, which makes it less prone to clotting, and means that it flows more easily through the arteries.

The Recipes

Sunrise

3 carrots
1 pear
2 cauliflower florets and
   stems
1 handful parsley

1. Trim the carrots.
2. Cut the pear into wedges.
2. Process all the ingredients in the juicer.

The Deterrent

4 apples
½ beetroot
sparkling mineral water

1. Cut the apples into wedges.
2. Process the apples and beetroot in the juicer.
3. Add mineral water to taste to add a sparkle.

The Red Refresher

225 g/8 oz red grapes
1 apple
75 g/3 oz cranberries

1. Remove the stems from the grapes if they are not organic.
2. Cut the apple into wedges.
2. Process the fruit in the juicer.

Spinach Surprise

6 carrots
4 spinach leaves
¼ green pepper

1. Trim the carrots.
2. Form the spinach leaves into balls.
3. Cut the green pepper into strips.
4. Process the vegetables in the juicer.

Sweet Ginger

5 carrots
1 pear
2.5 cm/1 in knob ginger-
   root

1. Trim the carrots.
2. Cut the pear into wedges.
3. Process all the ingredients in the juicer.

CHAPTER TWELVE

HIGH
BLOOD PRESSURE

The pressure of the blood is usually measured at two levels, the higher figure is systolic and shows the pressure of the blood leaving the heart as it contracts. The lower figure is diastolic, which is the pressure of the artery at rest. Basically blood pressure is the force generated by the blood within the system of arteries. A normal blood pressure reading should be about 120/80. Hypertension, more commonly known as high blood pressure, is usually regarded as a diastolic pressure over 90.

The underlying causes of high blood pressure can be factors such as disease – narrowing of the arteries, kidney problems, obesity and stress. High blood pressure is a problem because it is a potential killer, resulting in heart disease and strokes. A healthy diet is of course essential as a foundation, but in addition, a high ratio of potassium to sodium has been found especially useful in both preventing high blood pressure and in the treatment of the ailment. Recently, research studies have shown that increasing the consumption of foods rich in the minerals calcium and magnesium can be beneficial in a number of cases.

The Recipes

New Zealand Sunrise

1 pineapple round 2.5 cm/
   1 in thick
1 apple
3 Kiwi fruit

1. Remove the skin from the pineapple if it is not organic.
2. Cut the flesh into strips.
3. Cut the apple into wedges.
4. Process all the fruit in the juicer.

Cherryripe

125 g/4 oz cherries
175 g/6 oz black grapes
1 pear

1. Cut the cherries in half and remove the stones.
2. Remove the stems from the grapes if they are not organic.
3. Cut the pear into wedges.
4. Process all the fruit in the juicer.

Sprouting Success

6 lettuce leaves
1 pear
3 carrots
6 Brussels sprouts

1. Form the lettuce leaves into balls.
2. Cut the pear into wedges.
3. Trim the carrots.
4. Process all the ingredients in the juicer.

The Pressure Reducer

4 spinach leaves
5 carrots
4 watercress sprigs
½ handful of parsley

1. Form the spinach leaves into balls.
2. Trim the carrots.
3. Process all the ingredients in the juicer.

Take the Pressure Off

5 carrots
1 pear
4 broccoli florets with stems

1. Trim the carrots.
2. Cut the pear into wedges.
3. Process all the ingredients in the juicer.

CHAPTER THIRTEEN

FATIGUE

Have you ever woken up in the morning feeling tired and lethargic even after a good night's sleep? Most people have felt like this at one time or another. You just don't know how you are going to make it through the day ahead. But what makes it all the worse is the fact that you cannot seem to put your finger on the cause and thus are unable to cure the ailment. Often we put it down to being 'just one of those days' or it's our biorhythms that are not quite right. Maybe we've just got out of the wrong side of bed. I know that I have said this on more than one occasion.

Sometimes our lethargy can be self-inflicted by too many late nights, too much alcohol, overwork and worry. Burning the candle at both ends, in other words. There can be a physical cause of fatigue too. For example heart disease, anaemia, hormone problems and allergies to food and the environment are all factors to consider. However we justify it, it remains a common problem.

Unfortunately, it is a problem that can be self-perpetuating because when we feel tired we tend to lack the energy levels needed for any form of exercise. This means that our bodies' absorption of nutrients is impaired, leading to further drops in energy levels. Add to this the fact that we are not producing a chemical stimulant in our brains and the body is in a vicious cycle which becomes increasingly difficult to break. When we are in this tired state we tend to let our regular eating pattern go out of the window and live off snack foods which results in even fewer nutrients entering our bodies.

We need to break this vicious cycle by consuming energy boosting nutrients. The minerals zinc, magnesium, potassium and iron as well as the whole B vitamin group along with the vitamins C and E are all valuable in the fight against fatigue.

The B group of vitamins has an important role to play because it metabolizes fats, carbohydrates and proteins which are responsible for much of our energy. In fact, many athletes take increased amounts of B vitamins to enhance their performance. The vitamins C and E also contribute to vitality. You will notice rapid improvement by drinking juices rich in these nutrients because they are raw foods supplying important energy to your system.

The mineral iron keeps up our energy levels and iron deficiency leads to anaemia resulting in fatigue. Women, especially during pregnancy, and children are at most risk from anaemia. Magnesium is important in the metabolism of food resulting in energy production. Potassium is an essential activator for some enzymes, especially those concerned with the production of energy.

Whatever you do, do not reach for the biscuit barrel or cake tin for instant energy, as it will merely give you a very short-term lift, and you will need another sugary 'fix' in no time at all. Just drink the juices!

The Recipes

Alive, Alive O

3 spinach leaves
5 carrots
4 Brussels sprouts

1. Form the spinach leaves into balls.
2. Trim the carrots.
3. Process all the vegetables in juicer.

The Activator

4 carrots
½ handful parsley
6 sprigs watercress
2.5 cm/1 in knob of ginger-
   root

1. Trim the carrots.
2. Process all the vegetables io the juicer.

The Bouncer

2 pineapple rounds, 2.5 cm/
   1 in thick
25 g/1 oz spring greens
sparkling mineral water

1. Remove the skin from the pineapple if it is not organic and cut the flesh into strips.
2. Roll the spring greens into balls.
3. Process the produce in the juicer.
4. Add mineral water to taste to give a nice bubble.

Get Up and Go Juice

2 apples
2 celery sticks
4 asparagus stalks
2 tomatoes

1. Cut the apples into wedges.
2. Process all the ingredients in the juicer.

Go Go Juice

6 apricots
1 apple
¼ lime
6 lychees
4 Kiwi fruits
sparkling mineral water

1. Cut the apricots in half and remove the stones.
2. Cut the apple into wedges.
3. Peel the lime.
4. Peel the lychees and remove the stones.
5. Process the fruit in the juicer.
6. Add mineral water to taste to give a sparkle.

CHAPTER FOURTEEN

PRE-MENSTRUAL TENSION

Pre-menstrual tension affects most women at some time in their lives and can make life very miserable. It's not only the heavy stomach and back pains, it's the moodiness, weeping, anger and sometimes even violence that make life almost unbearable at these times. All the emotions seem heightened when suffering from PMT and behavioural symptoms can be very dramatic and totally out of character. It can, therefore, be quite alarming for the sufferer and her family. Increasingly it is being shown that dietary changes can have astonishing effects on PMT and in some cases the symptoms can be eliminated completely. That's great news for millions of women who suffer every month from PMT. There is also evidence to suggest that the same dietary changes can relieve the symptoms experienced during the menopause.

The nutrients to consume are the vitamins E and B_6 and the minerals zinc and magnesium.

The Recipes

Parsley Power

4 carrots
1 pear
4 cauliflower florets
½ handful parsley

1. Trim the carrots.
2. Cut the pear into wedges.
3. Process all the ingredients in the juicer.

Block Out Juice

4 carrots
4 spinach leaves
2 celery sticks
2.5 cm/1 in knob of ginger-
  root

1. Trim the carrots.
2. Roll the spinach into balls.
3. Process all the ingredients in
   the juicer.

The Tension Stopper

3 apples
2 broccoli florets with stems
4 watercress sprigs
½ handful parsley

1. Cut the apples into wedges.
2. Process all the ingredients in
   the juicer.

The Reliever

5 carrots
4 kale leaves
2 cloves of garlic, peeled

1. Trim the carrots.
2. Form the kale leaves into balls.
3. Process all the ingredients in
   the juicer.

Freedom Juice

1 carrot
4 apples
4 cabbage leaves
2 celery sticks

1. Trim the carrot.
2. Cut the apples into wedges.
3. Form the cabbage leaves into
   balls.
4. Process all the ingredients in
   the juicer.

CHAPTER FIFTEEN

STRESS
AND DEPRESSION

It is a long-established fact that what we consume can have a marked effect on our behaviour patterns and overall emotional state. Too much coffee and tea can make you depressed and unable to sleep because of the caffeine content. Too much sugar in your diet can provoke mood changes as the blood sugar level is disrupted violently.

I don't know about you, but alcohol can have a profound effect on my emotional state, and I don't have to consume much for it to take effect either. Whatever the mood I'm in, the alcohol will accentuate it. Whilst this is great when I'm in good spirits (excuse the pun), because I just become happier and happier, it is bad news when I'm not so happy. If I'm feeling sad I become increasingly depressed the more I drink. It's a very powerful medium which can turn some people from being gentle creatures into aggressive, angry monsters.

We are well aware these days of the effect certain foods can have on the individual. The hyperactive child is just one example. People can suffer from various mental and emotional disorders because of what they consume. Very often it is an inadequate intake of nutrients that is at the root of such problems.

Some of the symptoms associated with a deficiency in the mineral iron are depression, insomnia and a slowing of mental ability and agility. According to recent studies, iron deficiency is more common than was previously thought, and occurs mainly amongst women and children. In fact, 10 per cent of British women are classed as being anaemic, the ultimate test of iron deficiency. Vitamin C helps the body to absorb iron and so it is worth increasing your intake of this nutrient. Low levels of the mineral magnesium and the vitamin B complex are also associated with emotional and mental disorders.

Instead of reaching for the bottle of tranquillizers, uppers, sleeping pills or bottle of booze, why not reach for some of the juices that can give you a longer lasting boost and benefit your body into the bargain instead of destroying it.

The Recipes

The Smiler

225 g/8 oz Ogen melon
6 apricots

1. Remove the rind from the melon if it isn't organic and cut the flesh into strips.
2. Cut the apricots in half and remove the stones.
3. Process the fruit in the juicer.

Laughter Juice

4 apricots
125 g/4 oz raspberries
125 g/4 oz blackcurrants

1. Cut the apricots in half and remove the stones.
2. Process all the fruit in the juicer.

Live Wire

4 lettuce leaves
4 carrots
1 apple
3 Brussels sprouts

1. Form the lettuce leaves into balls.
2. Trim the carrots.
3. Cut the apple into wedges.
4. Process all the ingredients in the juicer.

Happy Days

4 apples
3 spring green leaves
1 handful parsley

1. Cut the apples into wedges.
2. Form the spring greens into balls.
3. Process all the ingredients in the juicer.

Sunshine Juice

5 carrots
3 spinach leaves
¼ green pepper
2.5 cm/1 in knob ginger-root

1. Trim the carrots.
2. Form the spinach leaves into balls.
3. Cut the pepper into strips.
4. Process all the ingredients in the juicer.

CHAPTER SIXTEEN

COLDS

A cold is a viral infection of the upper respiratory tract and is commonly referred to as cold in the head. The reason we seem to catch more colds in the winter months is not due to the colder weather but to the fact that we tend to stay indoors for longer in artificially-heated rooms that often have sealed windows and doors. The cold weather does not give you a cold but it can make you more prone to catching one by slowing down your blood circulation, making your immune system less effective.

It doesn't matter how healthy and fit you are, you will experience the odd cold from time to time. You cannot avoid them for ever. Some people, however, seem to catch cold after cold which is not only very unpleasant for the individual but is also unnatural.

There has been much research into preventing and curing the common cold. Vitamin C has been found useful in preventing catching a cold, whilst vitamin A and the mineral zinc are beneficial in alleviating the symptoms of the virus. So hope is not lost – start drinking the juices!

The Recipes

Citrus Zester

2 large oranges
½ lemon
½ lime
1 papaya

1. Remove the rind from the citrus fruits, leaving as much of the white pith as possible.
2. Break the fruits into large segments.
3. Peel the papaya.
4. Process the fruit in the juicer.

Cold Buster

1 large orange
1 grapefruit
sparkling mineral water

1. Remove the skin from the citrus fruits, leaving as much of the white pith as possible.
2. Break the fruits into segments.
3. Process the fruit in the juicer.
4. Add mineral water to taste.

The Sniff Stopper

1 mango
4 Kiwi fruits
176 g/6 oz strawberries

1. Peel the mango and remove the stone.
2. Process all the fruit in the juicer.

The Sneeze Zapper

3 tangerines
¼ lime
2 pineapple rounds, 2.5 cm/
   1 in thick

1. Peel the tangerines and lime and break into large segments.
2. Remove the skin from the pineapple if it is not organic and cut the flesh into strips.
3. Process the fruit in the juicer.

Dynorod

4 carrots
4 sprigs of watercress
2 cauliflower florets with
    stems
2.5 cm/1 in knob ginger-
    root.

1. Trim the carrots.
2. Process all the vegetables in the juicer.

Jungle Juice

4 carrots
3 spinach leaves
1 courgette
2 cloves of garlic, peeled

1. Trim the carrots.
2. Form the spinach leaves into balls.
3. Process all the vegetables in the juicer.

CHAPTER SEVENTEEN

OSTEOPOROSIS

Osteoporosis is a honeycombing of the bones due to loss of calcium in the body that is not replaced. It is responsible for bones becoming easily fractured and once fractured difficult to knot back together. Osteoporosis results in a loss of height as the backbone becomes compressed with the disease. This crippling disease is mainly associated with the menopausal and post-menopausal female. Women not only form less bone than men but they also lose it at a faster rate, especially during the menopause. This bone thinning disease affects one in four women in Britain.

It is widely accepted by the medical profession that a diet rich in calcium from childhood is important in the prevention of the disease. Many nutritionalists argue that increased calcium is required by the female after the age of thirty-five years to replace the increased loss of calcium from the body. Females reach their maximum bone mass at about thirty-five years of age and after this the bone building process slows down considerably and we gradually start to lose bone.

Exercise on a regular basis is also an important factor in preventing and treating osteoporosis. Women who lead sedentary lives or who are immobilized are at greater risk of contracting this condition.

Medical treatment of osteoporosis during the menopause and post-menopause is usually confined to hormone replacement treatment (HRT), with female sex hormones. Some doctors have found that they can give lower HRT doses if they include calcium in the treatment.

To prevent and treat osteoporosis by dietary methods you need to increase your calcium intake and your vitamin D intake, which will help absorption of calcium in the body.

The Recipes

The Bone Strengthener

4 carrots
6 sprigs watercress
¼ potato
½ handful parsley

1. Trim the carrots.
2. Process all the vegetables in the juicer.

Bone Power

3 kale leaves
3 apples
4 watercress sprigs
¼ cucumber

1. Form the kale leaves into balls.
2. Cut the apples into wedges.
3. Process all the ingredients in the juicer.

Bone Mass Builder

3 carrots
1 apple
4 broccoli florets with stems
1½ handful parsley

1. Trim the carrots.
2. Cut the apple into wedges.
3. Process all the ingredients in the juicer.

CHAPTER EIGHTEEN

ARTHRITIS

The major forms of arthritis are osteo arthritis and rheumatoid arthritis. Osteo arthritis is a degenerative joint disease resulting in loss of cartilage in the joints. It is characterized by calcified outgrowths from cartilage, eventually causing much pain and stiffness. Rheumatoid arthritis is caused by a disorder of the immune system. The membrane that protects the joint becomes inflamed and thickened. Stiffness, pain and swelling are experienced in many joints. Arthritis is a major cause of suffering, immobility and disablement.

The orthodox treatment is with drugs to reduce the inflammation and pain, or surgery to replace diseased joints may be resorted to when severe loss of movement and extreme pain arises. Many unorthodox treatments are used by the sufferers of arthritis – copper bracelets, acupuncture and diet. Avoiding red meat is advisable because of its high saturated fat content, and recent studies show a diet low in saturated fats to be beneficial to the arthritic. The nightshade family of vegetables, such as tomatoes, potatoes, peppers, aubergines and paprika should also be avoided as they can often cause joint pain. Other main foods that seem to exacerbate the symptoms of arthritis include dairy produce, refined carbohydrates, processed foods, oats and wheat. Both types of arthritis have been found to respond to the minerals calcium and selenium, and the vitamins nicotinic acid and vitamin C.

The Recipes

Joint Reliever

1 grapefruit
¼ lime
2 pineapple rounds, 2.5 cm/
   1 in thick

1. Remove the rind from the citrus fruits and break into segments.
2. Remove the skin from the pineapple if it is not organic and cut the flesh into strips.
3. Process the fruit in the juicer.

Stiffness Stopper

4 carrots
7.5 cm/3 in wedge of
   cabbage
2 celery sticks
1 clove of garlic, peeled
½ handful parsley

1. Trim the carrots.
2. Process all the vegetables in the juicer.

Mobility Juice

4 carrots
6 sprigs of watercress

1. Trim the carrots.
2. Process both the vegetables in the juicer.

Flexi Juice

3 apples
2 asparagus sticks
2 broccoli florets with stems
½ handful parsley

1. Cut the apple into wedges.
2. Process all the ingredients in the juicer.

Pain Reliever

175 g/6 oz Cantaloup melon
10 strawberries
1 Kiwi fruit

1. Cut the rind from the melon if not organic and cut the flesh into strips.
2. Process all the fruit in the juicer.

Loosen Up

2 pineapple rounds, 2.5 cm/
   1 in thick
4 carrots
3 broccoli florets with stems

1. Remove the skin from the pineapple if it is not organic. Cut the flesh into strips.
2. Trim the carrots.
3. Process all the ingredients in the juicer.

CHAPTER NINETEEN

DIGESTIVE PROBLEMS

Not many people go through life without suffering some kind of digestive discomfort. Quite often it can be something as simple as an upset stomach or heartburn which disappears in a day or two. Sometimes, however, it can be more serious, requiring medication and even surgery to cure the problem. The digestive process involves the dismantling of fats, proteins and carbohydrates in the food we consume into microscopic particles small enough to be transferred into the bloodstream. Our digestive system includes all the series of passages from the mouth to the anus. 'Digestive problems' is a blanket term covering a whole myriad of ailments such as ulcers, gallstones, appendicitis, constipation, upset stomach, heartburn, irritable bowel syndrome and diverticulitis.

When you consider how we constantly tend to abuse our digestive system it comes as no surprise that the system rebels and says 'enough'. We bombard our bodies with far too much fat, too many processed foods, too many additives and chemicals and not enough fibre. We then starve it of essential nutrients, vitamins and minerals, either by eating badly or whilst dieting to try to reduce our weight, having overconsumed calories. An all too hectic lifestyle, rushing around from A to B, skipping meals and existing off snack foods doesn't give our digestive system a chance.

The cure for the multitude of ailments that come under the label 'digestive problems' starts in the kitchen with a good healthy diet, and the emphasis is on fresh fruit and vegetable juices. The idea is to clear the body of toxic wastes that build up because of our bad eating habits. Drinking fruit and vegetable juices rich in folic acid and citrus fruits will do precisely this. And traditionally garlic, apples and lemons are all beneficial to any digestive disorder, whilst watercress, celery, cucumber and cabbage are great for relieving an acid stomach.

The Recipes

Mellow Yellow Juice

3 carrots
1 parsnip
2 apples

1. Trim the carrots and parsnip.
2. Cut the apples into wedges.
3. Process the ingredients in the juicer.

Exotic Cooler

4 tangerines
1 grapefruit
¼ lemon
1 papaya

1. Peel the citrus fruits, leaving as much of the white pith as possible.
2. Break the fruits into large segments.
3. Peel the papaya.
4. Process all the fruit in the juicer.

The Soother

3 apples
1 pear
¼ lemon

1. Cut the apples and pear into wedges.
2. Peel the lemon but leave as much of the white pith as possible.
3. Process all the fruit in the juicer.

Ease Out

½ fennel bulb
3 apples
7.5 cm/3 in wedge of cabbage
2 cloves of garlic, peeled

1. Cut the fennel into wedges.
2. Cut the apples into wedges.
3. Process all the ingredients in the juicer.

Melon Marvel

225 g/8 oz Cantaloup melon
50 g/2 oz red grapes
¼ lemon
1 apple

1. Remove the rind from the melon if it is not organic and cut the flesh into strips.
2. Remove the stems from the grapes if they are not organic.
3. Peel the lemon, leaving as much white pith as you can.
4. Cut the apple into wedges.
5. Process all the fruit in the juicer.

The Digestive Juice

3 pears
3 broccoli florets with stems
1 clove of garlic, peeled

1. Cut the pears into wedges.
2. Process all the ingredients in the juicer.

Citrus Calmer

1 large orange
1 grapefruit

1. Remove the rind from the fruits, retaining as much of the white pith as possible.
2. Break into large segments.
3. Process in the juicer.

The Cucumber Cure

3 apples
¼ cucumber
4 sprigs of watercress

1. Cut the apples into wedges.
2. Process all the ingredients in the juicer.

Vegetable Medley

3 carrots
7.5 cm/3 in wedge of
cabbage
2 celery sticks
1 clove of garlic, peeled

1. Trim the carrots.
2. Process all the ingredients in the juicer.

The Cure-All

3 carrots
1 parsnip
4 sprigs of watercress
1 handful parsley
¼ potato

1. Trim all the carrots and parsnip.
2. Process all the ingredients in the juicer.

CHAPTER TWENTY

GUM DISEASE

Gum disease, known as peridontal disease, is the most common cause of tooth loss. It is characterized by inflammation, bleeding and infection of the gum and underlying jawbone. The cause is thought to be food, bacteria and tartar deposits that lurk in the crevices between teeth and gums and are impossible to remove with a toothbrush alone. The bacterial infection progresses into the tissue and the gums eventually recede until healthy teeth loosen and fall out.

Recent research has shown that resistance to gum disease may be increased with a good diet rich in the mineral calcium. This can not only reduce the risk of developing gum disease, but can also reverse the condition in some cases. As well as calcium, the mineral magnesium and vitamin C have been found to have beneficial results, whilst bleeding gums are eased by the consumption of citrus fruits.

The Recipes

Healthy Gum Juice

¼ pink grapefruit
2 tangerines
¼ lime
125 g/4 oz strawberries
sparkling mineral water

1. Remove the rind from the citrus fruits but leave as much of the white pith as possible.
2. Break the citrus fruits into large segments.
3. Process all the fruit in the juicer.
4. Add mineral water to taste to give a sparkle.

Oral Fresh

3 kale leaves
4 carrots
2 cauliflower florets and
    stems

1. Roll the kale leaves into balls.
2. Trim the carrots.
3. Process all the vegetables in the juicer.

Pinky

4 spinach leaves
3 apples
1 pear

1. Roll the spinach into balls.
2. Cut the apples and pear into wedges.
3. Process all the ingredients in the juicer.

The Redundant Tooth Fairy Juice

4 carrots
¼ red pepper
6 sprigs watercress

1. Trim the carrots.
2. Cut the pepper into strips.
3. Process all the vegetables in the juicer.

Tooth Firmer

6 lettuce leaves
5 carrots
1 handful parsley

1. Roll the lettuce leaves into balls.
2. Trim the carrots.
2. Process all the vegetables in the juicer.

Berry Juice

125 g/4 oz raspberries
125 g/4 oz blackberries
175 g/6 oz strawberries

1. Process all the fruit in the juicer.

CHAPTER TWENTY-ONE

URINARY PROBLEMS

The urinary system concerns the kidneys and bladder, both of which manufacture and store urine until it is passed through the system. This essential process eliminates toxins and surplus water from the body. Some of the problems associated with the kidneys and bladder include cystitis, thrush, prostate problems, kidney and bladder stones, kidney failure and incontinence.

Any juice containing cranberries is a well tried and tested remedy for cystitis – the bane of many a woman's life. Asparagus, onions, cabbage, carrots, watercress, cucumber, celery and all leafy green vegetables are useful in combating most urinary problems. On the fruit front, try raspberries, watermelon, grapes, blackcurrants, redcurrants and gooseeberies. Juices are an ideal method of dealing with any urinary infection as it is essential to flush the system out by drinking plenty of liquids and what better way than with mouth-watering juices!

The Recipes

The Cranberry Cure

2 apples
1 pear
175 g/6 oz cranberries

1. Cut the apples and pear into wedges.
2. Process all the fruit in the juicer.

Ruby Juice

125 g/4 oz red grapes
75 g/3 oz watermelon
175 g/6 oz cranberries

1. Remove the stems from the grapes if they are not organic.
2. Remove the skin from the melon if it is not organic and cut the flesh into strips.
3. Process all the fruit in the juicer.

The Flusher

125 g/4 oz red grapes
1 apple
75 g/3 oz gooseberries
75 g/3 oz redcurrants

1. Remove the stems from the grapes if they are not organic.
2. Cut the apple into wedges.
3. Process all the fruit in the juicer.

The Cleanser

3 carrots
¼ cucumber
2 celery sticks
2 asparagus sticks
¼ small onion, peeled

1. Trim the carrots.
2. Process all the vegetables in the juicer.

Popeye choice

3 spinach leaves
4 carrots
6 sprigs watercress
1 clove of garlic, peeled

1. Form the spinach leaves into balls.
2. Trim the carrots.
3. Process all the vegetables in the juicer.

CHAPTER TWENTY-TWO

THE REST
OF THE STORY

The message from all interested parties, ranging from the government to the medical profession to the World Health Organization, concerning our eating habits is the same – we should all be following a healthier diet. And when I speak of 'diet' I mean the foods we consume each and every day, rather than a short-term weight-loss diet. Changing to a healthier eating pattern will result in weight loss for many people, naturally, and the weight will stay off because you are not caught in an 'on/off' diet situation. Healthy eating is a way of life and lasts for ever.

But then the burning question remains, 'What on earth is a healthy diet?' There is a consensus of opinion concerning the amount of fat and the types of fat we consume, how much fibre we eat, and the quantity of sugar and salt our diet contains. The foundation of any healthy diet depends on these crucial factors. Once this foundation has been laid, the building blocks of essential nutrients, vitamins and minerals, can be added.

We have to understand why certain foods are either good or bad for our health, otherwise we cannot hope to make the necessary changes because we are merely groping about in the dark. This chapter will give you the necessary information to make informed choices about the foods you consume and the foods you minimize in your diet.

The Fat Factor

---

*The amount of fat consumed by the average person should be
reduced by at least 15 per cent*

How many times have you wandered along a supermarket aisle and
been mesmerized by all the margarines, butters and low-fat spreads
that adorn the shelves. The choice is no longer just between
spreading butter or margarine on your bread. You have to consider
whether you want 'polyunsaturated', 'mono-unsaturated', 'unhydrogenated', 'hydrogenated' – and what about the fatty acids? All
these terms, and many more, are used by the manufacturers in an
attempt to gain your custom. The advertisement campaigners reflect
the health angle, boasting 'high in polyunsaturates' or '100 per cent
natural', we see healthy looking, happy families consuming certain
products and our subconscious mind forges the link between health
and their product.

It's very confusing to say the least, and it's not surprising that
many consumers are left scratching their heads and wondering which
product to buy.

The first point to make clear is that fats do not need to be
banished from the diet altogether. On the contrary, some fats are
essential to us – they are not all bad. It is the type of fat you consume
and in what quantities that will determine whether it is beneficial or
harmful to the body.

FACT FILE

Fat gives the highest energy of all nutrients

When we think of fat the first things that spring to mind tend to be
butters, margarines and oils. Then there is the fat you can actually see
on meat. These are easy to classify as fat because they are visible and

as such are relatively easy to monitor. It is the invisible fat a lot of foods contain that is much more problematic. Would you think of a peanut as fat? Just you try lighting one – most nuts are 50 per cent fat and will burn like candles. The coconut and avocado pear are 80 per cent fat. Even lean roast beef will contain about 11 per cent of its weight in invisible fat. And it doesn't stop there. Processed foods, most dairy products, chocolate, cakes, biscuits and crisps are all heavily laden with fat.

In the United Kingdom our average intake of fats amounts to 45 per cent of our total calorie intake. That's at least 15 per cent higher than it should be according to various dietary guidelines, including reports from the World Health Organization, the National Advisory Committee on Nutritional Education (NACNE) and Committee on Medical Aspects of Food Policy (COMA). No more than 30 per cent of our total calorie intake should be from fat. The type of fat is also important and this figure should be made up of no more than 10 per cent saturated fats, with the remainder being split equally between polyunsaturated and mono-unsaturated fats. All these figures and terms make the fat debate seem much more complicated than it actually is.

Saturated fats are a storage type of fat and provide us with a limited supply of energy. The consumption of saturated fat is unnecessary because our bodies can manufacture it if required from other nutrients such as protein and carbohydrates. Saturated fats also provide us with 'padding' and most of us feel we have too much of that already without adding to it.

The problem with eating too much saturated fat is that you store up health problems for the future and the risk of premature death. Saturated fats increase the level of cholesterol in the blood by encouraging the liver to make more. The cholesterol forms fatty deposits on the artery walls, making them narrow and restricting the blood flow. They may even become totally blocked. Saturated fat also causes the blood itself to become much thicker and stickier, making it more prone to clotting. Many serious diseases such as cancer, heart disease, strokes, high blood pressure, gallstones and diabetes are attributable to high intakes of saturated fat.

Polyunsaturated fats are a structural type of fat and perform many crucial functions in our bodies. In fact polyunsaturated fats are incorporated into every single cell in our bodies. It makes the blood thinner and less sticky, so less prone to clotting, and allows it to flow more freely through the arteries. This type of fat is essential if the brain and nerves are to develop and grow properly. It is crucial that this structural type of fat forms part of our daily diet as it cannot be manufactured by our bodies. Good sources of polyunsaturated fats are seed oils and fish oils.

Because the body cannot manufacture structural polyunsaturates, they are called Essential Fatty Acids and have been used in the management of certain diseases such as high blood pressure, cardiovascular disease, controlling cholesterol and alleviating the symptoms of pre-menstrual tension.

Mono-unsaturated fats have only recently entered into our thinking and we don't possess a great deal of information on this type of fat. However, research suggests that mono-unsaturated fats act in a similar way to polyunsaturates. The best sources of mono-unsaturates are olive oil and the fat found in poultry. It's a good idea to use olive oil if you have to fry something, as mono-unsaturated oils remain stable at high temperatures whilst polyunsaturates are unstable and quickly change to saturated fat. Better still use a dry-frying pan.

FACT FILE

Polyunsaturated oil should not be used for frying as it is unstable at high temperature and will gradually become saturated

---

Manufacturers boast 'high in polyunsaturates' on their cartons of margarine as they compete for custom under the healthy eating banner. Unfortunately, the consumer isn't necessarily getting what she or he thinks. Most of the margarines that use polyunsaturated fats would be liquid at room temperature, which would be a little messy for the consumer. It just wouldn't be practical. So the margarine is put through a process called hydrogenation. Hydrogen gas is added to any unsaturated fatty acids present in the oil and this changes the melting point, giving it a firmer texture at room temperature. Sounds good so far. But this process also makes the margarine saturated and thus unhealthy. Look for unhydrogenated on the margarine labels and if it states that it contains hydrogenated vegetable oils or hydrogenated unsaturated fats, don't buy it. At the present time only health shops stock unhydrogenated margarine.

And just to complicate matters further, there are those low-fat spreads that are becoming increasingly popular. Spreads are attract-ive because they are lower in fat and because they have fewer calories than their traditional counterparts. These spreads contain only 40 per cent fat, while by law, butter and margarine have to contain a minimum of 80 per cent. They can be a useful way of aiding weight loss and because they contain half the fat of butter or margarine you are reducing your intake of saturated fats automatically.

In reality it is easy to reduce the amount of fat you consume and to switch to a healthy unsaturated type once you are equipped with the knowledge to do so. After the initial effort it soon becomes an automatic process.

Fibre Facts

Fibre, or roughage as it used to be called, is a crucial element in any healthy eating plan and has been greatly underestimated for many years. Dietary fibre is what is left behind once our food has been digested and is turned into faeces. It plays an important role in our bodies by hastening the passage of food through the intestine, increasing the bulk of faeces and ensuring that it is produced more frequently.

According to all major research studies, we need to increase the fibre content of our diet. The NACNE Report, published in 1985, stated that our 'fibre intake should be increased by 33 per cent to 30 grams a day. This should come from increasing the consumption of wholegrain cereal, and fresh fruit and vegetables.' What was an important breakthrough in this report was that it didn't make these recommendations for people who were particularly at risk, but for the population as a whole. We are all at risk from the typical British diet.

People who don't eat enough fibre increase the risk of suffering from major diseases such as heart disease, various cancers, diabetes, diverticular disease, appendicitis, gallstones, obesity, haemorroids, hiatus hernia and constipation. All are thought to be preventable by increasing fibre consumption. And it is as easy as substituting unrefined foods for refined foods and eating plenty of fresh fruit, vegetables, beans and pulses.

There are different types of fibre and each plays a specific role in our body. The fibre we obtain from wheat and wholegrain cereals absorbs water from the gut, acting like a sponge in effect, and this helps to increase the bulk of the faeces. This type of fibre is helpful in relieving constipation. The fibre contained in lentils, beans and vegetables has been found to reduce blood cholesterol levels by absorbing it and helping its journey through the body. Generally speaking, fibre is fermented by bacteria in the gut and the by-products help to keep the large bowel healthy. The quicker the faeces pass through the body, the shorter the period of time that toxic substances are in contact with the walls of the colon, which reduces the risk of cancer. You need to gain your fibre from a variety of sources to ensure the full range of benefits fibre has to offer.

Dietary fibre is found in the leaves, roots, stems, seeds and fruits of plants. Nearly all vegetable foods contain some fibre, and the foods made with wholewheat, containing bran, are far richer sources of fibre than the refined milled types. Berries, such as blackberries and raspberries, contain higher levels of fibre than fleshy fruits such as apples; and dried fruits are excellent because the fibre is concentrated. Vegetables such as cabbage, peas and beans have the very best fibre levels relative to other vegetables.

It only takes a few basic changes to increase your fibre intake without disrupting your diet too much by having to make radical changes. Just by eating wholemeal bread you are consuming 350 per cent more fibre than by eating white bread. A good bowl of wholewheat breakfast cereal will give you over sixteen times the fibre of its refined counterpart, such as cornflakes.

Sweet Nothings

It is a fact that our diet in the western world, and specifically in the United Kingdom, contains far too much sugar. Although sugar consumption has been falling steadily since 1956, it still stands at somewhere between 75 and 100 grams (3–3½ oz) per day. According to the government's NACNE report, the maximum amount of sugar we should consume in a day is 54 grams. That is 10 teaspoons each day. Now I know that seems quite a generous amount because we tend to think of sugar consumption as the spoonfuls we drop into our coffee and tea. But, as you have probably guessed, the picture isn't as clear as that.

Approximately 60 per cent of our total sugar intake is accounted for by manufactured or processed foods. And I don't just mean sweet-tasting foods such as cakes, biscuits and jam. Tomato ketchup, for example, contains over 20 per cent sugar and most savoury foods contain sugar in surprisingly high quantities. So you can't simply halve the amount of sugar you add to your tea and coffee. It is the hidden sugars in a variety of foods which need to be tackled, and that can be harder than you think.

A quick look at the table below illustrates the problem well.

FOOD	AMOUNT	TEASPOONS OF SUGAR
Bran biscuit	1	3
Sparkling glucose drink	1 glass	7
Blackcurrant cordial	1 glass	6
Sugar-coated cereal	1 bowl	3½
Tinned fruit	1 small tin	5
Jelly	1 packet	19
Malted milk drink	3 tsp	2
Packet tomato soup	¼ packet	2
Baked beans	½ medium tin	2
Chocolate toffee bar	1	9

After looking at the table it isn't surprising that most westerners obtain too many calories from sugar. You soon reach your 10 teaspoons a day maximum limit. Let's face it, one glass of sparkling glucose drink and a bran biscuit and that's it.

Many a sweet tooth is developed in childhood with the help of well-intentioned adults who seek to make food more palatable for their children. Most children however will more than welcome the refreshing taste of fresh fruit without the 'enhancement' of sugar. The unfortunate thing is that once you have developed a sweet tooth, it is very difficult to get rid of it. Sugar is addictive and if you are used to sugar, your taste buds will not take kindly to unsweetened drinks and foods. However, do persevere because after a week or two your taste-buds will adapt and you will appreciate the real, true flavour of food and drink instead of just the overpowering sweetness. Kicking the sugar habit is the best thing you could do for your looks as well. Your eyes will be brighter, your complexion clearer and smoother, and you will have lost a few pounds into the bargain!

The problem with sugar is that it is totally devoid of nutrients – it gives nothing but 'empty' calories. Demerara sugar retains some of the colour and flavour of raw cane sugar, but it is little better than white sugar in terms of nutrients. Other brown sugars are merely white sugar tinted brown with caramel or some such syrup.

When you consume sweet foods have you ever noticed how quickly you want more? This is because the satisfying feeling of being full soon vanishes with such foods, and within a short space of time we need more. Sugar really does encourage us to overeat and become obese because sugary, high-calorie foods do not fill our stomachs effectively. It becomes a vicious circle that is increasingly harder to break.

Sugar consumption has been linked to serious diseases such as diabetes, heart disease and cancer. But the picture remains controversial. Research continues – watch this space! However, there is no doubt that sugar causes tooth decay, especially when it is consumed in a sticky form such as toffee. Tooth decay is a serious risk to general health for as well as causing problems with teeth and gums it can lead to digestive problems.

Salt

Research studies indicate that our western diet contains too much salt. In fact, we need to at least halve the amount we consume. A 'normal' diet supplies about 12 grams of salt per day – ideally it should be no more than 5 grams.

Salt is the main source of sodium in the diet, and high sodium consumption is strongly associated with strokes, heart disease, stomach cancer and high blood pressure.

Unfortunately, as with sugar, salt is a cheap and plentiful commodity which is valuable to manufacturers as a flavour enhancer and preservative. So much of the salt we consume is hidden from us in processed foods – in fact, about 75 per cent! Breakfast cereals have added salt, as do most tinned vegetables, tinned meats and tinned fish. Then there are the obviously high salt foods such as crisps, salted nuts and other snack foods.

As with sugar, it is better to reduce your salt consumption gradually to allow your taste-buds to adapt.

INDEX